D1334979

Prayer
MADE

AUTUMN

HOUSE

Prayer
MADE
PRACTICAL

GOD
at close quarters

FREDERICK
PELSER

Copyright © 1996 by Frederick C. Pelser

First published in 1996

ISBN 1-873796-65-X

Printed and published by
Autumn House,
Alma Park, Grantham, Lincolnshire,
NG31 9SL, England

3 5 7 9 10 8 6 4 2

Prayer MADE PRACTICAL

CONTENTS

Only by prayer

The sun was hardly up when they started coming — men eager not to miss a word, women in excited groups; wide-eyed youngsters. Hundreds soon hemmed Him in on all sides.

He did not raise His voice, yet the quality of resonance carried every syllable to the listeners farthest away. Though the words were simple and direct, there were elements of intonation and emphasis, a quality of gentleness, a loving tenderness, that affected them like the cadences of music. They were impressed by what He was saying, but at the same time were so charmed by Him as a speaker that when they came to tell their friends these things that evening, they would unconsciously use the same inflections and gestures.

As the day wore on, the crowd grew to thousands. New-comers now were mostly physically handicapped or sightless people led by the hand. Before midday Jesus stopped speaking in order to heal the hundreds who needed help; and exclamations of joy echoed from the hills. Then, with not a single sufferer in His audience, He resumed His teaching.

So eager was the throng for more insights that there was no time to eat. As the sun began to set and people turned reluctantly homeward, some women pressed bread and fruit on Him. 'You must be starving!'

At last they were gone in the gathering dusk. He thanked God for the food and ate. They were all snug in their homes now. Imagine the exuberance and thanksgiving there must have been where blindness, disease or other abnormalities no longer weighed the spirits down!

While in the surrounding towns they slept, Jesus made His way by moonlight into the hills, knelt in a selected spot, and started praying. At times His voice was a quiet murmur, blending with the sounds of the night; at other times it rose in urgency, or fell silent in meditation. Always it was marked by earnestness, a heartfelt sincerity.

His whole night passed in prayer. In the early glimmer of light which was nothing more than a lessening of the darkness, His disciples found Him and overheard His words. They stood spellbound. There was no formality here, no pompous or hackneyed phrase; but something so intimate, so replete with love and trust and praise, so unselfish in pleas on others' behalf, that the disciples felt it was beyond their understanding. In all the thousands of prayers they had voiced since childhood, they knew they had never begun to achieve such heights of the spirit, such a reaching out of the soul. This was a sublime, intimate conversation between two Persons, the One visible, in each other's immediate presence.

'"Lord," said one, "please teach us to pray!"'[1] There was something desolate in his voice, an acknowledgement that his whole prayer life until this moment had lacked heart and soul and understanding. His friends waited, eager, ready to discover a new world.

More than 500 years earlier the prophet Daniel had learned the divine science of prayer. It had become the soul of his religious life. He could as soon stop breathing as stop praying. The Lord of his life wanted this remarkable fact to become known to the universe and to history. To this end, He allowed certain scheming men to have their way.

Daniel's enemies in government, with jealous eyes on his political position, were desperate to find fault with him. But 'they could find no corruption in him, because he was trustworthy and neither corrupt nor negligent.'[2] Finally they agreed that they would never find any basis for charges against Daniel unless it had something to do with his religious life.

'He'll pray to his God, regularly and often, even if doing so were to cost him his life!'

With that settled, it was only a matter of getting King Darius to issue a decree testing every citizen's loyalty. Almost overnight it became law that for the next thirty days anyone who directed a petition to any god or man except the king would be thrown into the lions' pit.

When Daniel discovered what had been done behind his back, there must have been a moment of incredulity. This strange law could be aimed only at him. His private life must have come under the scrutiny of his influential enemies. No one could see him on his knees in his room before daybreak each morning, or observe his bedtime prayers, or the times when he rose in the middle of the night to pray. Even less could anyone tell that he unswervingly practised continuous prayer, unbroken communion with God, in the midst of pressing government business here in the palace in Babylon. If he went on with continuous prayer no human could be any the wiser. When it came to private kneeling prayer, all he had to do was keep clear of windows.

But it was known that he took a break in the middle of the day to visit his upstairs prayer room. Just entering that prayer room meant prayer, breaking the king's decree. Would he keep away from the prayer room?

Daniel looked at the shadow cast by the sun. It was time!

He left his office and crossed the courtyard, knowing that eyes were on him. In his apartment he went up to the roof and entered the prayer room. Here was the west-facing window in front of which he invariably knelt . . . there was the cushion for his knees. From the flat roof nearby he would be perfectly visible. Would he compromise, shift the cushion to left or right, hide behind the blank wall? For just thirty days make it impossible for anyone to prove that he had prayed to God?

He knelt, as always, at the open window. His voice was humble, low, clear. Three men came out on the flat roof, saw him and heard his words, then hurried off with their report.

When the soldiers came to arrest him, Daniel was waiting for them.

At the lions' pit hours later the king said remorsefully, 'Daniel, I'm sorry! I've tried everything I could think of to save you. Surely, *surely*, the God whom you are forever serving will somehow save you . . . I can't.'

The roar and growl of the lions was blood-chilling. Minutes later Daniel was among them — and not one harmed him. All through the long hours of the night, touched, rubbed against and sniffed by the lions, he conversed with his heavenly Father in gratitude and awed wonder.

When the grey light of dawn spilled into the exposed part of the den, he heard King Darius's voice, muffled and urgent,

'Daniel! Daniel! Can you hear me, Daniel? Was the God whom you're always serving able to save you?'

He was hauled out, the man who would rather die than give up his praying.

Why did the Redeemer of mankind feel He needed prayer? How could He spend entire nights in prayer? Saying or doing what, to fill up so many hours? Why did something in His overheard prayer so profoundly stir the disciples' souls? Did Jesus have prayer secrets?

Why did Daniel feel he could not afford to miss even one of his daily prayers?

Why do people pray, and why should they pray? What is effectual prayer? What are the hindrances to effectual prayer?

Do you want things to go your way in prayer . . . or not necessarily?

The science of prayer can be learned. It must be mastered by everyone who is determined to make a success of his life.

'See Luke 11:1. ²Dan. 6:4.

Why do people pray?

It was an exciting day on the vast sheep farm. To see the endless flocks of sheep grazing peacefully; sheep being dipped and dosed and, after dark, to see by the headlights of cars locusts being poison-sprayed was a memorable experience for a city dweller.

There were some unpleasant moments along the way. Such as when the father and eldest son lost their tempers with each other and nearly came to blows. And the swearing. These were people who were in a Christian church every week.

The eldest son and I retired to his room at about 1am. I was in bed first, saw him switch off the light, heard him hop into bed. Then he was out of bed, kneeling, mumbling a prayer. 'Why did you do that?' I asked before breakfast.

'I must,' he replied. 'That's how I was taught. That's how my mother brought me up. It's just part of me.'

And that is *reason number one* why so many pray, in Christianity and in Islam and in other religions. They do it because this is how they were taught. They have been conditioned to say their prayers. Parents have moulded their children; praying is a habit, part of the child's culture. Yet that child might never really get to know God.

The Hebrews in Old Testament times paid close attention to the training of their children. 'These commandments that I give you today are to be upon your hearts. Impress them on your children. Talk about them when you sit at home and when you walk along the road, when you lie down and when you get up!'[1] They grew up praying, and in turn trained their children. Yet God told Israel, 'When you spread out your hands in prayer, I will hide my eyes from you; even if you offer many prayers, I will not listen.'[2]

How horrified Israel must have been when the prophet Isaiah told them how God disdained their prayers! Prayers are not acceptable to the Creator if they are no more than a pious habit, a bit of culture or tradition, a convention.

There is a second reason why people pray.

In March 1989 Michelle Hamilton of Australia set out in a tiny rowing boat from Boracay, one of the islands of the Philippines. She wanted to go round a spit of the island, have a picnic, then row back to the cabin she and her mother shared. The tide was deceptive and her blaring radio mind-numbing, and it took an hour or more before it dawned on her that she had been swept into a fast ocean current. She was alarmed, switched off the radio din, and set to work to stroke back to the island.

The sea was turning choppy. Straining with the effort, wheezing and groaning, she tried to make each stroke count, turning to gauge her distance from time to time. With a sense of disbelief she saw more than five hours pass. The island was farther away than ever. She exclaimed to herself, 'This boat is a death trap!' She stood up to dive into the sea to try swimming to the island. Then she saw the dangers — sharks, darkness soon to fall, a storm about to break. She collapsed, whimpering. The island was too far, receding too fast. In the grip of such a powerful current she'd have no chance.

Soon the storm and the night were upon her. Waves towered over her, then flung her and the boat violently into the air. Once she found herself sucked down, down. She battled to hold her breath, to claw her way up. Her boat was gone . . . no, it had capsized. She found an outrigger and clung to it all through the night as the waves boiled and crashed about her and flung her about like flotsam.

Then she began to pray. Earnestly, desperately, the cries tore from her. 'Help! Help! God, if You're out there, help!' She could not hear her voice above the fury about her.

She drifted for three days and two nights, without sleep or water, holding on to a boat which she could not right. She saw sharks and prayed and they did not turn towards her. She saw a fishing vessel and prayed, but there was no one on deck to spot her waving arm. She kept praying and then two men appeared on deck and one saw her. The boat slowed down and came to rest about one kilometre away. They gesticulated for her to swim to them. In a daze of exhaustion and prayer she did so. The Fishing Vessel *Alyss* at last took her on board, where she sank down on the deck and through a tortured throat sobbed to the captain, 'Thank you for saving my life!'

'I didn't save you,' he replied. 'Surely you must realize it was God who saved you?'

Michelle's twenty-two years had been empty of God, empty of religion. Storm-tossed and drifting southwards, alone on the vast Pacific, she learned something about prayer to God. Why did she pray? Because she *wanted something* — protection from the waves and sharks, energy to keep going, rescue.

The second reason why some pray is therefore — they want something. It could be prayer for money or something money can buy; or for health, friendship, achievement in education or sport, a marriage, a holiday. They know the Bible says, '"Ask and it will be given to you"';[3] so they have set their hearts on something and hope prayer will deliver it.

People whose prayer life is motivated by a selfish desire do not know what prayer is.[4] Nor do they know the Creator of the universe, the Sustainer of every particle of matter and every vestige of life. Without knowing God, they can't truly pray.

Now, the third reason.

Some pray because they are *afraid*.

Life is full of dangers — crime, illness, AIDS, viruses, population explosions, crop failures, air pollution, holes in the ozone layer. People feel they might end up like Job saying, '"What I feared has come upon me; what I dreaded has happened."'[5] They need an amulet, a lucky charm, a lucky prayer to ward off the dangers. Not praying would make life even more perilous.

So people pray because they have been taught that this is the thing to do, or because they want something, or because they fear. It is right to teach others to pray, to approach God with our needs and fears. But our motivation for having a prayer life should be higher, nobler.

The reason for prayer and a prayer life should be: 'I want to get closer to my God. I need God with every fibre of my being. I want total intimacy, an all-pervading relationship with Him. I want to become more like my heavenly Father. I want the Holy Spirit to rule my life. As Paul says, I want to die to myself, and have my life "hidden with Christ in God!" [6]

Jesus says that He wants us to be 'in' Him, 'one' with Him. [7] This suggests much — knowledge, a cherished Bible, correct understanding of the Bible, obedience as a way of life; private prayer and continuous prayer as a way of life. It involves a living, growing faith. 'I want to know Christ and the power of his resurrection and the fellowship of sharing in his sufferings, becoming like him in his death.' [8]

How Christ's heart must overflow in tenderness when He sees someone who has these motives! Man needs hundreds of things for life and eternity. But he has an insatiable urge to pray for one great reason — to revel in God's presence and will. He says, 'Lord, because I love You I can't stay away from You. Please hold me. May Your presence be a spring of water in me, "welling up to eternal life". [9] Don't let my heart wander from You. Help me to love You and live night and day with You . . . .'

The Holy Spirit stands ready to cultivate in us the right prayer motives, and to teach us to pray. [10]

---

[1]Deut. 6:6, 7. [2]Isa. 1:15. [3]Matt. 7:7. [4]James 4:3. [5]Job 3:25. [6]Col. 3:3. [7]John 17:21. [8]Phil. 3:10. [9]John 4:14. [10]Rom. 8:26.

Confession

Marilyn got out of her car and wondered if she had enough money. She checked, reassured herself, and shut the car door. As she was turning away a chilling thought struck her. She peered anxiously through the driver's window — yes, there were the keys, dangling in the ignition lock! She had locked the keys in the car!

'Mark,' she was soon saying to her husband from a phone in the supermarket, 'I feel terrible! I've locked the keys in the car. What am I going to do? Do you have the spare set?'

'I do,' he admitted without enthusiasm. 'But I'd have to go right across the city to get them to you . . . .'

'Oh, Mark, *please!*'

He sighed. 'I'm very busy, in the middle of something . . . . Oh, I suppose I'd better drop everything. But it will take me at least forty minutes.'

She leaned against the car, assailed by thoughts of self-recrimination. After thirty minutes her eye fell on something. 'No, it can't be!' she exclaimed, and reached a trembling hand to a back door. It *was* unlocked!

She felt embarrassed, guilty and foolish. All this time Mark had been battling his way through the traffic. When he arrived and found the car unlocked what would he think? With a guiltily pounding heart she quickly locked the back door.

Mark arrived, sweaty and rushed. He soon had her car open and she found herself saying, 'I don't know what I'd have done without you!'

The rest of the day she was unhappy with herself. At dinner she felt an urge to tell him about the unlocked rear door, but could not muster the courage. The hours and days dragged past. When Mark was particularly considerate she felt more stricken, false. After three days she realized that unless she put this right her conscience would never give her peace.

She confessed — confessed that she had failed to check the other three doors before jumping to a conclusion, then had locked the back door to hide her omission. 'And then, when you came I played a role, pretended to something untrue, left you under a false impression. I'm so abysmally sorry! I was a fool and a coward! Can you ever forgive me?'

With her confession and his forgiveness she felt a new person, able to live with herself once more.

Confession *is* good for the soul. It has its place not only in human relations but in prayer.

The Creator has always had a problem with getting humans to own up to their guilt. When Cain murdered his brother Abel he had no conscience about the matter — even blithely denied it. The Lord set the prophet Jeremiah searching high and low in Jerusalem for *one* honest, faithful person — but he found none.[1]

The Holy Spirit reads our hearts. There is no secret action, or even thought or desire, hidden from Him.

Look at the character of God. 'Just as he who called you is holy, so be holy in all you do; for it is written, "Be holy, because I am holy." '[2] You and I know that we are not holy; we'd never call ourselves holy. 'All have sinned and fall short of the glory of God'.[3]

What are the principles against which we stand guilty?

1.   The first of the Ten Commandments is broken by all people. It demands that God be supreme in our lives. I do not set myself first in my life — God is first. I don't belong to myself. I am His. I don't do, eat, drink, think what I like. His Spirit and character must reign in me! His will is my pleasure.

2.   Command Two requires spiritual, direct worship; not an easy outward religion but one that demands my heart, my all.

3.   I must totally honour and reverence God.

4.   I must keep holy His holy day.[4] It is a symbol of His sanctifying me.[5] The holy Sabbath of God can be kept only by someone who is being sanctified by the Holy Spirit.

5.   I will respect and honour all authority placed over me by God.

6. I will reverence life and do my utmost to preserve and enhance it.

7. I will be pure in thought and action.

8. I will be honest in thought and act.

9. I will be truthful in thought and act.

10. I'll be content, not envious.

We are going to be judged in heaven's court. To allow us to escape judgement, Jesus took our sins upon Himself when He died for us.

I can now plead His love, purity and death, asking for forgiveness — and instantly receive it!

What are your sins? Have you confessed them lately? Have you shed the burden of guilt, been given a new start, a new lease of life?

Daily at least some of our praying will be confession of sins — things we've done, things we should have done. These will be mentioned by name. We'll say, 'Father, I do not deserve forgiveness. I deserve only death. I hate and detest my sin, and come in the name and merits of my Lord Jesus Christ to ask forgiveness. This forgiveness You have promised in Your word. By faith I accept it. Thank You eternally for pardoning me.'

The promises are there. 'If we confess our sin, he is faithful and just and will forgive us our sins and purify us from all unrighteousness.'[6] '''I have swept away your offences like a cloud, your sins like the morning mist.'''[7] 'As far as the east is from the west, so far has he removed our transgressions from us.'[8] '''None of the sins he has committed will be remembered against him.'''[9]

If that prayer is sincere and earnest, it is heard and answered. Where we have harmed someone else, we should admit that to the person concerned and ask his or her pardon. We'll make no confession that will harm others. Where we have caused someone to suffer loss, we will try to make restitution. In these things our sincerity will become clear. No human being can grant us absolution; but our heavenly Father can and will. Our faith can grasp it and rejoice. Our faith will rest not on the presence or absence of certain emotions but on faith in God and His Word.

'He who conceals his sins does not prosper, but whoever confesses and renounces them finds mercy.'[10]

One of the rich privileges of prayer is sorrow for sin and confession with the consequent forgiveness. Then 'we have peace with God through our Lord Jesus Christ'.[11]

---

[1]Jer. 5:1. [2]1 Peter 1:15. [3]Rom. 3:23. [4]Gen. 2:1-3; Exod. 20:8-11. [5]Ezek. 20:12. [6]1 John 1:9. [7]Isa. 44:22. [8]Ps. 103:12. [9]Ezek. 33:16. [10]Prov. 28:13. [11]Rom. 5:1.

Spiritual prayers

Prayer happens when a human speaks to the Creator.

What does he say to his Creator?

He may say, 'Lord, I appreciate You. You are great, the Lifegiver. Yet You are willing to listen to me! This is mercy — and love! How much I admire Your power, wisdom and infinite knowledge. And the exalted love of which You are the Source! Thank You for being who You are and what You are. To worship You is my greatest privilege . . . .' This would be a prayer of *adoration*, a very exalted kind of prayer.

Other prayers can be characterized by *confession* of sin. Or be mainly for others — *intercessory* prayers. Or they can be prayers of *thanksgiving* — an outpouring of the heart for untold visible and invisible blessings.

Most prayers are *request* prayers. Things are asked for. In fact, this is the only kind of prayer known to most people. 'Give me food. Give me money. Give me health. Keep me safe. Keep me warm in cold weather.'

In comparison with adoration, request prayers sound petty, selfish. Yet all kinds of prayers are important, and this is no less true of request prayers. God urges that we put our requests to Him. '"Ask . . . seek . . . knock."'[1] '"What do you want me to do for you?" Jesus asked the blind man who replied, "Rabbi, I want to see." "Go," said Jesus, "your faith has healed you." Immediately he received his sight and followed Jesus along the road.'[2]

Our requests to God can be of two kinds — for the things of our temporary life, and for spiritual things. *Temporal prayers* are prayers for things like food, clothing, shelter, protection, recovery from illness, matters of friendship or marriage, the comforts of life.

'"The pagans run after all these things, and your heavenly Father knows that you need them."'[3] 'The pagans run after all these things' shows that temporal needs can be an obsession; the prayer life can easily become unbalanced; spiritual realities and priorities can be lost. Yet our Father knows we need food, shelter and such things, and He cares. He wants us to bring such needs to Him.

' "But seek first his kingdom and his righteousness, and all these things will be given to you as well." '[4] 'His kingdom and his righteousness' denote our spiritual needs — forgiveness, the Holy Spirit, fruits of character such as self-control, faith, strength, humility, and a strong and intimate prayer life. These all reach beyond our death; they mean eternal life to us. If we have true priorities we'll concentrate our request prayers more on our spiritual needs than on our temporal needs.

After all, immortal life is immeasurably more attractive than the human life-span.

The experience of Gavin throws an interesting light on *spiritual prayer*. He was a very winsome character — a sincere smile, bright, friendly, boyish blue eyes and a firm handshake. Everyone loved him in the church which he attended at least once each week. His frank, open face inspired confidence. Sometimes there was a hint of sadness in his eyes, as when his first marriage ended after a year.

When the second marriage lasted little longer and the two ex-wives implied that his character was seriously flawed, there were shocked stares. He was so palpably the perfect gentleman. While the two who had shared his life said unkind things about him, he spoke of their virtues and assumed the blame. This made him more trusted than ever, and it soon became evident that another lady of the church would welcome becoming Mrs Gavin III.

He seemed to be holding off. He had good reason to. He had a secret life, lived out of sight of his church friends. In the circle he frequented, sexual things were dominant. Gavin had grown up preoccupied with sexual fantasies. Away from the church folk, he fed his fantasies with his reading and entertainment. Sensuous images even possessed his mind at church during prayers.

There were times when he told himself that he was a scoundrel, and a rogue; and he tried to reform. Some of his struggles were so severe that he cried out for help; but soon he was in the back alleys once more, laughing and joking.

A public evangelist visited the city. Gavin attended the meetings and heard things from the Bible that startled him. With self-critical motives he started studying his Bible and reluctantly came to the conclusion that he had important decisions to make. He did make them. One of these involved believer's baptism. After he had been baptized he found that he was involved in an intense struggle with himself over his secret life. Months passed and feelings of helplessness, self-condemnation for repeated betrayals of his resolves, and something like despair convinced him he should get counsel. The evangelist was back in the city for a few days; he went to him.

'I see,' said the evangelist after listening for twenty minutes. 'And you have tried to break away from your sin?'

'I have. I read from John 14:14: "You may ask me for anything in my name, and I will do it." I pleaded. No result. Then I prayed, "Lord, take away my sin *if it is Your will*." Once again, nothing. Thirdly, I asked many others to pray for me, saying I had a bit of a problem, nothing more. I thought if others held me up in prayer I'd get the victory. I didn't.'

The evangelist was lost in thought for a while, then handed Gavin writing materials.

'You'd better jot down the points I am about to make. Number one, gather all the texts in the Bible that have a bearing on your sin. Ponder them prayerfully. Make sure you know how guilty you are in God's sight — *His* view, *His* will in the matter.

'Number two, *kneel* in prayer before your Maker. Speak quietly, reverently, audibly. The sound of your voice will help your mind to concentrate and not wander. Number three, *confess* your sins and guilt. Make no excuses. In the presence of God, be honest with yourself.

'Number four: Pray, "Lord, it *is* Your will that this sin be overcome." You know beyond all doubt that it is God's will to get the victory. By saying, "Lord, *if* it is Your will, give me the victory" you'd be denying the teachings of God's Word. You'd be toying with God! You don't want to do that. Be honest. This principle holds for all spiritual duties. I'm talking about *spiritual prayers*, which are not about material things like a car or a job or food. Spiritual prayers are about the spiritual things God promises you, and the spiritual things He requires of you.

'Now number five. You plead, ''Father, deliver me *now*. Not some day — now, to the honour of Your name. To that end I surrender my heart to You now.'' Number six: Remind yourself of 1 John 1:9: ''If we confess our sins, he is faithful and just and will forgive us our sins and purify us from all unrighteousness.'' Believe this! Say, thank You, Lord, You have pardoned me and will purify me . . . . Accept that by faith in His Word. Number seven: Give thanks! Rejoice in God's grace.

'Number eight: Go and live your prayer. Don't leave it to the Lord to act out your prayer for you. You must do it, in His power. Number nine: Avoid temptations, situations that will compromise your faith. Even watch your thoughts. Resist and reject idle daydreaming. Prayerfully watch yourself.

'Number ten: Tell your friends you have been made into a new person by the Holy Spirit. Number eleven: When you weaken, send up a flash prayer for help. Number twelve: If you stumble, get up and go resolutely forward.'

Gavin was impressed. He spent days consulting the Bible, collecting pronouncements against his sin until at last he cried out, 'I'm lost! I'm my own worst enemy!' Point by point he studied the prescribed procedure. He made every decision. It was hard to keep off the enchanted ground of temptation. At times he experienced anguish and despair and had to plead for extra grace. Sobs and cries were not absent from his bedroom.

He won through. A new Gavin emerged, more thoughtful, a man of his word, neater even in his personal habits. By prayer his feet had been set on the path of sanctification, without which no one can hope for immortality;[5] and by prayer he was enabled to remain on that path.

He became noted for the zeal with which he was always trying to share the light he had received from heaven. His tireless witnessing bore fruit in conversions. I saw a man baptized who poured out words of thanks to a joyfully tearful Gavin as they embraced each other.

It became Gavin's burden to explain things to people. 'There are two kinds of prayers: spiritual and temporal. Temporal prayer has to do with our needs during this brief life. Spiritual prayer concerns our fitness for heaven — faith in God, obedience to every teaching of God's Word, forgiveness of sin, power to overcome, a deeper devotional life, the grace to reflect the character of Christ more fully, a life yielded to the Holy Spirit, obedience to the moral law. All these blessings are promised to the sincere and earnest seeker. He knows God's will, claims God's promises, thanks God, and lives his prayer with divine help! I know. That's how God saved me! Saved by God's grace, the Christian's main burden in prayer is that his life might glorify his Lord. He wants to seek first God's kingdom and righteousness.'

At Gavin's funeral about five years later I said to someone, 'There goes a true child of God.' 'Yes!' came the emphatic response. Then, referring to 1 Thessalonians 4:16, 17 and Revelation 20:6, he said, 'When the Lord descends from heaven to raise the dead in Christ and they rise to everlasting life, Gavin will be among them!'

We stood looking down into the open grave, thanking God for His marvellous salvation.

---

¹Matt. 7:7. ²Mark 10:51, 52. ³Matt. 6:32. ⁴Verse 33. ⁵Heb. 12:14.

Temporal prayers

Psalm 145 offers marvellous assurances and promises. 'The Lord is good to all; he has compassion on all he has made.'[1] This goodness is seen in many ways: arable soil, rain, crops, food, oxygen to breathe, companionship and a thousand other blessings. Above all, at great cost to Himself God has made provision for every person who turns to Him with all his heart to receive an endless, happy life.

Moreover, 'The Lord upholds all those who fall and lifts up all who are bowed down.'[2] 'You open your hand and satisfy the desires of every living thing.'[3] He is a prayer-answering God for 'He fulfils the desires of those who fear him; he hears their cry and saves them.'[4]

Such promises lift our spirits and put a new gleam in our eyes. Read in disregard of the context of the entire Bible, they could lead us to conclude that true followers of the Creator have no problems! And if difficulties do arise, all they need do is pray and all is well.

The Lord's promises, correctly understood, can be utterly relied upon. Yet there are lessons to be learned and characters to be developed in the course of this brief probationary life.

Take Aunt Zelda, a faithful soul, a true believer. When it was found that the tumour in her head was malignant she took it calmly. Just one thing disquieted her — she was sure her husband was not ready to meet his Maker. He needed spiritual help daily . . . needed it desperately. She decided to pray that what medical science could not do for her the Lord would do.

She knew that faith was vital, and read in Mark 11: ' "Have faith in God," Jesus answered. "I tell you the truth, if anyone says to this mountain, 'Go, throw yourself into the sea,' and does not doubt in his heart but believes that what he says will happen, it will be done for him. Therefore I tell you, whatever you ask for in prayer, believe that you have received it, and it will be yours." '[5]

With a calm earnestness typical of her, she started asking

for healing, ending each petition with, 'Lord, I believe that You have answered my prayer and healed me. Thank You, dear Father.' But the bulging tumour did not disappear.

After a week and at least twenty prayers, she began to doubt the quality of her faith. She knew that faith with many was a state of excitement, tension; there could even be moans and loud shouting. Perhaps that was real faith? She asked the Lord to help her, and set herself to work up her emotions.

She never felt comfortable with loud shouting, which seemed to imply deafness or reluctance on God's part; but for two weeks did manage to become so wrought up that she groaned, panted for breath, and felt quite sick afterwards. The tumour remained.

She knew that prayer requests were to be made in the name of Jesus Christ, and ended each prayer with that formula. She pondered the words, ''I will do whatever you ask in my name, so that the Son may bring glory to the Father. You may ask me for anything in my name, and I will do it.''[6] The thought came to her that perhaps she should use the name of Jesus oftener in each prayer — repetition might bring about what one mention failed to do. So she began to attach the name of Jesus to each sentence, sometimes each phrase.

This gave her a happy glow; but as the days passed there was no indication that the cancer was being cured.

She sat staring at James 5:14-16 for hours, then spoke to her young minister. The result was that an anointing service was held in her home. She believed she would be healed, and was perplexed when this did not happen.

Reading a booklet on prayer she came across phrases such as, 'Prayer bends the arm of God', which made her feel that her prayers were very deficient. Perhaps other Christians would be more effective? She decided to ask for intercessory prayer. After all, the Bible says if two believers join in a request, the result is guaranteed.[7] Aunt Zelda would go one better. She asked *two churches* to pray for her.

Time passed with no ray of light to cheer her. An older minister who had taken over visited her and she told him everything. He was impressed with her. There was no querulousness, no questioning of God's ways, just a measure of confusion and a tendency to blame herself for not understanding true prayer.

This minister invested time in her problems and eventually offered these thoughts: First, faith was vital, but should not be identified with emotionalism. Faith was not a state of tension, excitement, but calmly believing God's Word. Faith was trusting God's character and loving spirit, and His wise judgement.

All who want to show true faith in the course of their praying should remember Mount Carmel. The 450 priests of Baal were to pray that fire might descend on their offering. They started with voices of shuddering earnestness, sibilant intakes of breath, moans, fulsome praise of their gods, cries. They bombarded the gates of their mythological heaven.

They worked themselves up in an orgy of emotion. Nothing came of it.

Then Elijah prayed. There was no emotionalism. He was not wrought up, vehement, insistent. He simply said, 'Let it be known that You are God and I Your servant and that You are turning their hearts back to You.'

At once flames of fire, like brilliant flashes of lightning, descended from heaven, consuming the sacrifice, licking up the water in the trench, and even consuming the rocks of the altar.

The Lord was teaching a lesson. Faith is not noise and sweat and hoarseness. Satan might indeed respond to emotionalism, posing as an angel of light to confuse and destroy.[8] No, faith is a quiet, fervent trust in God.

A second time the Lord underscored that vital lesson. When a hurricane tore the mountains apart 'the Lord was not in the wind'. Then 'there was an earthquake, but the Lord was not in the earthquake. After the earthquake came a fire, but the Lord was not in the fire. And after the fire came a gentle whisper'.[9] And God was in the whisper! Vehemence and emotionalism are presumption, a form of self-worship; the 'whisper' carries true, humble faith.

Second, the minister went on with his explanation, the statement about throwing mountains into the sea by faith was figurative language. Never at any time did the Lord Jesus fling a literal mountain into the sea, although He had such power. But He triumphed over the numerous 'mountains' which Satan raised to hinder His work. In the same way God would remove apparently insuperable problems which Satan placed in the way of true believers.

Third, what is meant by praying 'in the name of Jesus'? This is not a formula, especially not a *magic* formula. To pray in the name of Jesus means to pray in His spirit, with His purpose, asking what He would have asked. Such prayer is not intended to change God's mind or purpose or decision. It is intended to bring us into harmony with God's mind.

'Aunt Zelda,' said the minister, 'through Christlike prayer we do not expect that God's arm may be ''bent'' or ''twisted''. Never! We pray that God's *will be done*. We trust our heavenly Father completely. Is that clear?'

'Pastor, you've given me a lot to think about,' Aunt Zelda observed. 'I can see that faith should not be based on emotions. Of course, I knew about the priests of Baal on Mount Carmel. But when you're in trouble you tend not to think — how shall I put it — calmly, judiciously. Hope takes over and can make one's thinking unbalanced, off beam. Then, the mountain in the sea. Yes, that must be a figure of speech. And praying in the name of Jesus, meaning in His spirit, the mind of Jesus . . . that's a deep thought. I did know it, but it had got vague in my memory. Jesus did not pray selfish prayers. He prayed for others. It's hard to find an instance where Jesus prayed for something for Himself. Did He ever?'

'Yes, He did, Aunt Zelda. Remember in Gethsemane when His soul recoiled from the contamination of taking our sins on Him? He prayed, ''Take this cup from me.'' Then He added, ''Yet not my will, but yours be done.'' '

'I remember. So, no insistence, ever.'

'Well, there I'd like to be a little careful. When I ask that a sin be forgiven I know that I'm asking the very thing that is God's will. If I ask for victory over a sinful habit I'm asking in harmony with God's will. I should not say ''if it is Your will'', but ''thank you, Lord, for giving me the victory,'' and I must set myself in faith to live accordingly.

In all spiritual requests we can say, ''Lord, You promised in Mark 11:24 that whatever I ask for in prayer and believe that I receive it, will be mine.'' In spiritual prayers we claim God's promises. But in our temporal prayers it's different.'

There was a smile on her lips. 'Like my healing,' she said.

'Like your cancer, yes. We do have temporal needs — food, shelter, security, companionship, intellectual fulfilment. About these things Jesus says, ''Is not life more important than food, and the body more important than clothes?''[10] The main thing is everlasting life, and the things that pertain to it — faith, love, sanctification. But our temporal needs, though subordinate, also concern our heavenly Father — ''your heavenly Father knows that you need them''.[11] Jesus assures us of God's total interest: ''Even the very hairs of your head are all numbered.''[12] The needs of our fleeting days we are also invited to bring to our Lord in prayer: ''Give us today our daily bread.'' ''[13]

'But we've got no blank cheque?' she suggested.

'No blank cheques,' he smiled. 'Otherwise no Christian will ever be ill or jobless. Unbelievers would say, ''Christians have no problems; it would pay us to join them.'' Soon their ranks would bulge with the unconverted and self-seeking. And the Christians would get soft in character, weak, unfit for God's kingdom.'

'There's a purpose in suffering,' Aunt Zelda said with conviction and a gleam in her eyes.

'Undoubtedly! The Bible says, ''We must go through many hardships to enter the kingdom of God.''[14] To claim that our temporal prayer will always be answered in the very way we wish it, and for the very thing we want, is presumption. God knows what is best for our character, our everlasting life. As one celebrated writer put it, ''The purification of the people of God cannot be accomplished without their suffering.'' God in all-knowing wisdom reads our past, present and future. He answers our prayer in the light of what would be best for us. God is too wise to err, and too good to withhold any good thing ''from those whose walk is blameless.'' ''[15]

'That's how I prefer it!' Aunt Zelda exclaimed. 'I don't want a God who can be pestered or bluffed, badgered or shamed into yielding to my erring will.'

'Tell me, Aunt Zelda . . . if you could get the cancer removed in an instant by insisting, by dictating to God, or you could leave the final decision in God's hands — which would you do?'

'Pastor . . . it would be a relief to be rid of the cancer. Health is my greatest gift in this life. I've gone through a lot of anguish; I can't deny it. But . . . God is good. He has my best interests at heart. Jesus gave His life for me. If my Father, knowing the future, sees that the best thing for my character and preparedness for eternal life and the intimacy of my relationship with Him is healing . . . then I'm sure He'll heal me. And then? I must die eventually. In a year's time? With spiritual lessons unlearned, needing to be learned? In torment? I don't want that!' She considered for a while. 'No, if I could insist on the healing and get it instantly, I'd rather not. I want the Lord to decide. ''To me, to live is Christ and to die is gain'', as Paul said. I feel much, much safer in God's hands than in my own, Pastor.'

He swallowed, deeply touched by her spirit. 'Aunt Zelda,' he said fervently, 'surely goodness and love will follow you all the days of your life, and you will dwell in the house of the Lord for ever!'

'Amen,' she responded, blinking away a tear, relishing the words of Psalm 23.

She was such a bright spirit. She gave more than she received when she was visited. She talked to the nurses and visitors in her careful, considered way about the love of God. She prayed with and for people who were unhappy.

Then she very quietly slipped out of this life. In her funeral service we thanked God for the divine miracle of her life, her total faith in her heavenly Father.

---

[1]Ps. 145:9. [2]Verse 14. [3]Verse 16. [4]Verse 19. [5]Mark 11:22-24. [6]John 14:13, 14. [7]Matt. 18:19. [8]2 Cor. 11:14. [9]1 Kings 19:11-13. [10]Matt. 6:25. [11]Verse 32. [12]Matt. 10:30. [13]Matt. 6:11. [14]Acts 14:22. [15]Ps. 84:11.

Paul's greatest challenge

In Nepal they call it *Sagarmatha* (the Summit of the Skies); in Tibet it is *Chomolungma* (the Goddess Mother of the Earth). Mount Everest inspires that sort of salute. It challenges the imagination. The British mountaineer George Mallory wanted to climb it 'because it is there', and the epigram became famous. In pursuit of Everest's mystique he was last seen, in the company of his climbing partner Andrew Irvine, approaching the summit, which is 8,848.7 metres above sea level (29,028 feet). That was in 1924. Their bodies were never recovered.

Edmund Hillary and Tenzing Norgay first scaled Everest's summit in 1953. In 1978 Reinhold Messner and Peter Habeler became the first to scale the summit without taking along oxygen.

But a greater experience, more universal and eternal in its challenge, had to be faced by the Apostle Paul.

What an unusual man he was! In imagination we see the brilliant scholar in Jerusalem. 'Come and hear this strange man, Jesus,' someone urges. Paul glares at him. 'Never! I am expecting the true Messiah. Under no circumstances will I honour this deceiver and charlatan with my presence. Never will I set eyes on him!'

See him later on his way to Damascus with warrants for the arrest of followers of Jesus. Suddenly a light blazes in the sky above him, brighter than the midday sun, blinding those eyes that had scorned to look at Jesus. A voice thunders down, '"'Saul, Saul, why do you persecute me?'"' Flat on the ground, Paul fights for breath to gasp out the words, '"'Who are you, Lord?'"' and in a daze hears the words, '"'I am Jesus.'"'[1]

Then Paul becomes history's most remarkable champion of Christ. Aflame with zeal for the Master, he employs his mastery of numerous languages[2] to light the fires of the faith in many countries. And God honours him in uncommon ways.

In Iconium the Holy Spirit uses Paul not only to preach but also to perform 'miraculous signs and wonders'.[3] At Lystra he heals a crippled man, lame from birth.[4] At Philippi he heals a girl possessed by a dark spirit. At Ephesus God works singular miracles through Paul so that when handkerchiefs or scarves which have been in contact with his skin are placed on the sick they are rid of their diseases.[5]

At Troas Paul held a farewell meeting. He was so burdened with things to share with his audience that he spoke until midnight. In that upstairs room a young man named Eutychus was sitting on a window ledge. He fell asleep and toppled to the ground below. He 'was picked up for dead'.[6] Paul went down, undoubtedly shocked and prayerful, and clasped Eutychus in his arms, and the people 'took the boy away alive'.[7]

On the island of Malta Paul helped to build a fire to dry out the survivors of a shipwreck. As he handled a pile of brushwood a deadly viper came out and sank its fangs into his hand. 'This man must be a criminal getting his just deserts!' the natives exclaimed. 'But Paul shook the snake off into the fire and suffered no ill effects. The people expected him to swell up or suddenly fall over dead, but after waiting a long time and seeing nothing unusual happen to him, they changed their minds and said he was a god.'[8]

Publius, the chief official of Malta, introduced Paul to his father, who 'was sick in bed, suffering from fever and dysentery. Paul . . . after prayer, placed his hands on him and healed him. When this had happened, the rest of the sick on the island came and were cured.'[9]

A man of phenomenal faith, we would say, with a towering gift of divine healing. But God's dealings with people are complex.

Paul's prayers for his sick friend and colleague Trophimus brought no healing. He left him behind ill at Miletus.[10]

Nor did Paul's faith, gift and prayers bring healing in respect of his own physical problems. Didn't Paul know how to pray? Did he lack faith? Didn't he truly know God?

This man was especially called by God. 'While they were worshipping the Lord and fasting, the Holy Spirit said, "Set apart for me Barnabas and Saul for the work to which I have called them." '[11] When Paul was flogged and put in prison with his feet in stocks and at midnight praised God with joyful hymns, God showed His regard for His servant and delivered him by means of a violent earthquake.[12] Paul denied himself and committed himself daily to God — 'I die every day — I mean that, brothers.'[13] '"I have been crucified with Christ and I no longer live, but Christ lives in me. The life I live in the body, I live by faith in the Son of God, who loved me and gave himself for me." '[14]

Yet this man of undying faith and unswerving dedication, whose prayers God answered in the healing of so many, was left unhealed!

Some believers find this idea repugnant. One morning in Indiana I walked into the television station where I was making a series of evangelistic videos, and paused to listen to a radio sermon coming over a loud speaker. The preacher was emphasizing Psalm 103:3. 'When people tell you it may not be God's will to heal you, don't listen to them! The Bible says it IS God's will to heal ALL your diseases! He heals all your diseases! That's His will! When the sick pray and say, "Heal me if it is Your will", they are denying the Bible! They're denying faith! They're listening to Satan! God gives you His personal promise: He will heal all your diseases. Claim the promise! Say, "God, I take You at Your word. You have given me this solemn promise to heal all my diseases. You can't lie! At this instant, perform this promise for me, heal me in Jesus' name!" '

How would the great Apostle Paul, denied healing by God, have answered this healer-preacher? He would have said, as Peter did, that the Bible is sometimes distorted by people 'to their own destruction'.[15]

In Psalm 103 King David devotes the first five verses to musing to himself about God's blessings to him. He does not want to forget what God has done for him. He enumerates his blessings, so that they will be fresh in his memory and will serve as a testimony to others. For extra clarity we turn to the

New English Bible: 'Bless the Lord, my soul; my innermost heart, bless his holy name. Bless the Lord, my soul, and forget none of his benefits. He pardons all my guilt and heals all my suffering. He rescues me from the pit of death and surrounds me with constant love.'[16]

God had cured David of his spiritual diseases, his guilt. When he prayed, 'Wash away all my iniquity and cleanse me from my sin,'[17] God had cleansed him. When he prayed, 'Create in me a pure heart, O God, and renew a steadfast spirit within me,'[18] God had granted him new life, new grace to live a spiritual life.

In the same way, God had restored him to physical health every time he had been sick, so that he was alive and able to sing God's praises. In the fourth verse David praises God for preserving his life from the 'pit of death'. Later, of course, he became ill and God permitted him to die.[19]

Paul would not lift Psalm 103:3 out of its context and present it to sick people as a blank cheque from God: 'Every time any believer is sick, I'll heal him.' That would be cruel. David sets us a noble example in Psalm 103 by testifying, 'God has forgiven my sins, healed me of my spiritual and physical diseases, and protected my life.' Every follower of Jesus will give the same witness as long as he lives.

We all die. The faith healers get sick and die. A correct understanding of the divine science of prayer can bring sufferers inexpressible peace and joy in the Lord.

How did the saintly Paul handle his problem? It was a physical problem — 'a thorn in my *flesh*'.[20] Using figurative language he calls it a 'thorn' and a 'messenger of Satan, to torment me'. What this tormenting condition was is not as important a lesson to us as Paul's responses.

Paul's first response: On three occasions in his life Paul made his malady a matter of special prayer. In answer, God revealed Himself. He made it clear that He would not answer Paul's prayers by granting the healing. He would do so in another way — by giving Paul strength to bear the problem and triumph over it.

Paul's second response: He accepted God's 'No' in a way that takes one's breath away. 'Therefore I will *boast* all the more gladly about my weaknesses, so that Christ's power may rest on me. That is why, for Christ's sake, I *delight* in weaknesses . . . in difficulties. For when I am weak, then I am strong.'[21]

The greatest challenge to Paul had been in accepting God's will when He said 'No'. Not only did he accept it — he rejoiced in it! He might have insisted on healing. He might have marshalled his host of converts to Christianity to bombard the gates of heaven with intercessions, trying to 'wear God down', to 'bend God's arm', to bring God over to Paul's will: 'Heal me!'

Instead he set an immortal example in submitting to God's will, in rejoicing in God's 'No' decision and assurance of sustaining grace. The lesson is clear.

True faith says, 'Father, You can do anything. Furthermore, You are good, kind, loving, feeling everything I feel. I know that You will do for me what I ask, or immeasurably more than all I ask or imagine, according to Ephesians 3:20. Whatever Your loving and wise decision, I know that is what I would have chosen if I had known the end from the beginning. Make me staunch and true, rejoicing in You and honouring Your name as long as I have breath.'

[1]Acts 26:12-15. [2]1 Cor. 14:18. [3]Acts 14:3. [4]Verses 8-11. [5]Acts 19:11, 12. [6]Acts 20:9, NEB. [7]Verse 12, NEB. [8]Acts 28:5, 6. [9]Verses 8, 9. [10]2 Tim. 4:20. [11]Acts 13:2, emphasis ours. [12]Acts 16:16-40. [13]1 Cor. 15:31. [14]Gal. 2:20. [15]2 Peter 3:16. [16]Ps. 103:1-3. [17]Ps. 51:2. [18]Verse 10. [19]1 Kings 2. [20]2 Cor. 12:7, emphasis ours. [21]Verses 9, 10, emphasis ours.

The true spirit of prayer

When we pray we are not speaking to a human being. The most intelligent person on earth has, compared to the Creator of the universe, no thinking ability. In prayer we are addressing the Being who made our sun and keeps it blazing. And how many other suns did He call into existence by His mental power? Astronomers tell us that the total number of stars, or suns, in the universe is something like the total number of grains of sand on all the seashores of the world.

Try to get a mental picture of that number. How many grains of sand does a child scoop up in its beach bucket? How many scoops of the bucket are needed to remove all the sand from one small beach? How many beaches big and small and patches of wave-driven sand are there on planet Earth?

And each grain of sand represents one gigantic sun! And each sun is in orbit, moving at a terrifying speed with an awesome precision.

But life, intelligent life, is God's ultimate miracle. He made the eyes reading these words, and the brain behind those eyes. He sustains that thinking brain and pulsing life moment by moment. It is a miraculous sustaining. Without it, like a light switched off, you would cease to be.

Our heavenly Father assures us '"As the heavens are higher than the earth, so are my ways higher than your ways and my thoughts than your thoughts."'[1]

Before this Majesty you — how appropriately — go on your knees. How will you talk to Him? With *awe* and *reverence*.

The Lord Jesus told of a supplicant who was 'justified before God'. When he started praying, 'He would not even look up to heaven, but beat his breast and said, "God, have mercy on me, a sinner"'.[2] He realized how small he was in God's presence, how stumbling and erring man's brain is. More, he realized how devoid of purity and goodness he was in the sight of the Holy One of the universe.

He utterly *needed* God; that he knew beyond any doubt. ' ''Apart from me you can do nothing,'' ' says Jesus.[3] This is the spirit in which to start praying.

A *sense of unworthiness* is appropriate. Job said, ' ''I despise myself and repent.'' '[4] 'Come, let us bow down in worship, let us kneel before the Lord our Maker.'[5] Often when praying we marvel that the Great One gives us audience. Surely the Almighty is astoundingly humble and loving to honour us with His attention.

'The Lord is the great God,' our hearts will sing as we kneel in our place of private prayer, alone with our Maker. 'In his hands are the depths of the earth, and the mountain peaks belong to him. The sea is his, for he made it, and his hands formed the dry land.'[6] 'Lord, I praise You — I owe my life to You. And You have paid with the life of my Lord to pardon my sins and give me endless life.'

In awe and reverence we *adore* the Loving One who said, 'You may call me your Father.' 'How great is the love the Father has lavished on us, that we should be called children of God!'[7]

Prayer should also be *sincere*. It should come from the heart. Ideally it is not read or recited but spontaneous. It should be meant.

'We've made it phoney by not really meaning what we say when we pray,' a young London student said. It's like the two small children walking home hand in hand after Sunday school. The little boy said to the little girl, 'Do you believe in God?' She replied, 'What will He do to me if I say ''No''?' Many say what they think God wants to hear — to curry favour with Him, to try to appease Him by making the right sounds.

They might even adopt a 'prayer language', such as automatically saying 'Dear loving and heavenly Father' instead of, 'Dear Father'; saying, 'I beseech Thee' when they would have liked to say, 'I ask You'; saying, 'I repent of all my iniquities' instead of, 'I'm sorry for this sin.'

Some who have the prayer habit cling to known sin. 'If I had cherished sin in my heart, the Lord would not have listened.'[8] Known wrongs must be righted; we must hide ourselves in the worthiness of Christ.

Others seek signs from the Lord. 'If I find my missing keys today, that will mean You are going to answer my prayer for the healing of my sciatica.' Chance things — a telephone call, a letter in the post, the weather clearing. We should not mark out some particular way in which the Lord should work for us. Trust God implicitly; live by faith.

' "True worshippers will worship the Father in spirit and truth, for they are the kind of worshippers the Father seeks." '[9] Truth demands *sincerity*. Prayer is honestly opening the heart to our heavenly Father as to our best, most trusted, most understanding Friend.

People can be sincere yet cold, unmoved, detached; so the Lord says worshipping 'in spirit' is important. *Earnestness* is required. When I was young in the ministry I took a veteran minister, since deceased, to a believer who was about to undergo a major operation. She asked us to pray for her. I was astonished at the formal, uninvolved, distant tone of my colleague's prayer. This prompted me to pray as though it was I whose life was about to hang in the balance. The appreciation in the patient's eyes was unforgettable.

Without our shouting, deliberately working up our emotions, or the frenzy of fanaticism, our prayers should be *earnest*, with heart and spirit in them.

Sincerity and earnestness should help us to *persevere* in our prayers. 'Jesus told his disciples a parable to show them that they should always pray and not give up.'[10] Sin is always forgiven the moment we sincerely and earnestly confess the sin and ask for pardon; but in other matters there might seem to be a delay, testing our faith and affording it a chance to grow by exercise. If we really believe that our request is unselfish and to the glory of God, we should not allow ourselves to grow weary and lose interest. A spirit of perseverance — which is the opposite of impatience — is part and parcel of real prayer.

God says, ' "Ask and it will be given to you." '[11] But He does *not* say, 'Ask *once* and you will receive.' Unwearyingly persist in prayer. The persistent asking brings the petitioner into a more earnest attitude; he becomes a deeper person. Self-knowledge increases; a spirit of dependence on God grows.

Faith is another factor in real prayer. Faith sees God as a Person of supreme reality; faith is a relationship of obedience to Him. Faith makes us passionately eager to obey God at all costs. It is not an emotion, a feeling; it is a principle, a set of the mind. When we come to Him in faith every petition enters the heart of God.

Our Father's love and wisdom guarantee that He puts our best interests first. A boy pleaded with his father for a bicycle. His dad tried to explain why he was saying 'No': 'Your balance is not yet as good as it should be. I've seen you fall when kicking a ball. I've seen you run into a tree when the ground was uneven. Some day I'll buy you a bike, when I'm sure it won't bring you pain.' The boy was glum and self-pitying. He even told a friend, 'My dad is against me.'

People are constantly asking for things they would not plead for if, like God, they were all-seeing and all-knowing. Should God give them everything they ask for? Children who get everything can become spoilt, selfish and undisciplined. Love demands that God consult His wisdom. How would getting this affect their character — its purity and strength? How would it affect their soul — closeness to God, growth in grace and love, spiritual maturity, prayer life? How would it affect their influence, example, witness — would it make them more pungently 'the aroma of Christ among those who are being saved and those who are perishing'?[12]

Even while we are praying our whole future in time and eternity is open to God. He knows exactly what will be *best* for us and others. This is what He decides — it is His will for us.

This means one of two things: One, it might be exactly what we asked for. In that case, at the right time the Lord grants it. Or, secondly, in mercy He may say 'No' to our request, but will answer our prayer according to His wisdom, in our best interests. The prayer is not lost but will bear fruit. We honour God by faith; and He promises, ' " "Those who honour me I will honour." ' "[13]

For many people there are two matters concerning which it is particularly difficult to pray 'Not my will, but Your will be done.' One is romance and marriage; the other, illness.

'But, Mother, I love him. And he loves me.' Jeanette exclaims. Her mother sighs, tired. How hard she has tried to explain about compatibility in culture, religion, habits. 'You don't really know him, child.' 'Oh, but I do, I do.' 'How can you be sure it is God's will for the two of you?'

Jeanette could not see how such an exciting and immortal love could not come from God. But not quite ten years later she said to me, 'I thought I loved him. Actually, I hate and detest him. Sometimes I've had to fight the urge to plunge my scissors into his neck. My mother was right, I hate to say. It was never God's will.'

In terminal illness it is a severe test of one's trust in God to pray, 'If healing me would not be to Your highest honour and my long-term best interests, please do not heal me.' There are surprisingly many who are enabled to do this. They would not for a moment think of themselves as heroic, courageous. Yet they cling to Christ and refuse to turn a request into a demand. 'God is good, too good!' they say. 'His will be done!'

A man said to his wife, 'I trust you. You are so loyal, so whole-hearted, never changing, constant, loving. You are fallible, a human being. Yet I know you always seek what is best for me.'

Our heavenly Father is like that — but He is infallible, 'the Father of the heavenly lights, who does not change like shifting shadows'.[14] 'You will keep in perfect peace him whose mind is steadfast, because he trusts in you.'[15]

---

[1]Isa. 55:9. [2]Luke 18:13, 14. [3]John 15:5. [4]Job 42.6. [5]Ps. 95:6. [6]Verses 3-5. [7]1 John 3:1. [8]Ps. 66:18. [9]John 4:23. [10]Luke 18:1. [11]Matt. 7:7. [12]2 Cor. 2:15. [13]1 Sam. 2:30. [14]James 1:17. [15]Isa. 26:3.

A vital concept

'What is prayer to you? How do you see prayer?' Christians were asked.

Replies were: 'Oh, prayer is . . . I recite the Lord's Prayer.' 'Prayer is . . . well, I think of God. I remember to say "thank you".' 'Prayer is talking to God.' 'Prayer is telling God my troubles and asking His help.'

A New York newspaper carried the item, 'PRISON FOR HIS NOISY PRAYERS. Pastor Wilbur M. Simmons has been sentenced to two months' imprisonment at Macon, Georgia, on charges of "making too much noise while worshipping."' Another view on prayer comes from the 1990s: 'A clergyman wants to start a "pay-as-you-pray" scheme to lift his church out of the red' — the church being St Aldate's church, Gloucester.

All very interesting — but what *is* prayer?

True prayer is not necessarily formal or noisy; nor is it vague, or a commodity with a price tag. It is the sincere and earnest opening of the heart to the heavenly Father in trust, in spontaneous words.

This is a marvellous arrangement. God does not need our prayers, because there is nothing we can tell Him that He doesn't already know. Because our prayer is spontaneous, we don't always know in advance precisely what we'll say. God does — He knew each word before we were born!

Yet He wants us to come. 'Take with you words, and turn to the Lord,' He urges.[1] Come and unburden your heart. '"Come to me, all you who are weary and burdened, and I will give you rest."'[2] It goes beyond comprehension, the love that moves the Creator to listen while we talk.

More is involved than our words, however. At its most glorious, prayer is a two-way conversation. We speak to God, and wait on Him to reply by the movings of the Holy Spirit on our hearts.

There is a strange blessing in this. In our 'closet' prayers, alone with God and not pressed for time, we can fall silent and give the Holy Spirit a chance to make our slow minds receptive to God's voice.

This is a vital concept. '*Wait* on the Lord: be of good courage, and he shall strengthen thine heart: *wait*, I say, on the Lord.'[3]

This brings to mind the well-known scripture: ' "*Be still*, and know that I am God." '[4]

Dr Andrew Murray, whose books *Abide in Christ* and *With Christ in the School of Prayer* have blessed many, said, 'If the question be asked whether this be anything different from what we do when we pray, the answer is that there may be much praying with but very little waiting on God. In praying we are often occupied with ourselves, with our own needs, and our own efforts in the presentation of them. In waiting upon God the first thought is of the God upon whom we wait. We enter His presence and feel we need just to be quiet so that He as God can overshadow us with Himself. God longs to reveal Himself, to fill us with Himself. Waiting on God gives Him time in His own way and divine power to come to us.' — *Waiting on God*.

As is to be expected, the Psalmist knew about waiting on God. 'Truly my soul silently waits for God; from Him comes my salvation. . . . My soul, wait silently for God.'[5] 'Be still before the Lord and wait patiently for him.'[6]

The supreme example for the Christian, in prayer as in everything else, is Jesus. And He spent hours waiting on the Father. 'Now it came to pass in those days that he went out to the mountain to pray, and continued all night in prayer to God.'[7] Did He occupy the entire night uttering words, without repeating Himself or getting drowsy? How did He spend eight hours or more at prayer? By meditation; by waiting on the Father.

His mind was saturated with the Scriptures. Even as a youth Jesus seemed to know the Old Testament Scriptures from beginning to end. So great was His spiritual knowledge as an adult that educated people exclaimed, ' "How did this man get such learning . . . ?" '[8] As He spoke to His Father and then reflected on the Word, waiting on God while His mind reached out in faith, the mysterious wonder occurred.

Soul knit with soul, and the Father and the Son were in communion. From these audiences He always emerged refreshed and knowing His Father's will.

'''No one ever spoke the way this man does,''' people on occasion exclaimed about Him.[9] So remarkable was His conversational life with His Father, that His disciples clamoured to be trained by Him in prayer.[10]

Waiting on God cannot be hurried. The flower must unfold by itself from the bud. Moreover, the one who loves God and relishes communion with Him wants to linger over this kind of prayer. 'Closet' time brings such peace, joy and fulfilment: it revives the spirit and restores the soul.

Experience has taught that such prayer is facilitated by the reading of the Word of God which prepares the mind for prayer. During the waiting time in the prayer, it helps to read a passage on the life of Christ, or a psalm, then to meditate on it. Another aid to keeping the mind focused is a favourite hymn. Let's take an old-fashioned example; Charles Wesley's 'Jesus, Lover of My Soul'. Depending on circumstances it can be sung or recited:

Jesus! Lover of my soul, let me to Thy bosom fly,
While the billows near me roll, while the tempest still is high:
Hide me, O my Saviour, hide, till the storm of life is past,
Safe into the haven guide: O receive my soul at last!

Other refuge have I none, hangs my helpless soul on Thee;
Leave, O leave me not alone, still support and comfort me:
All my trust on Thee is stayed, all my help from Thee I bring;
Cover my defenceless head with the shadow of Thy wing.

Thou, O Christ, art all I want, more than all in Thee I find!
Raise the fallen, cheer the faint, heal the sick, and lead the blind:
Just and holy is Thy name, I am all unrighteousness;
Vile and full of sin I am, Thou art full of truth and grace.

Plenteous grace with Thee is found, grace to pardon all my sin;
Let the healing streams abound, make and keep me pure within:
Thou of life the Fountain art, freely let me take of Thee,
Spring Thou up within my heart, rise to all eternity.

Only the Holy Spirit can teach the art of prayer. 'Lord, teach me to pray' is a petition that should often have a place in our prayers. Prayer is the holiest exercise of the soul. As we reach out to God in our private prayer-life and in continuous prayer, something dynamic is being done in us by the Holy Spirit. We are learning, changing, deepening; particularly as we learn to wait on God.

A sincere soul named Ann confided, 'My husband Jim is a very successful professional man. A good provider, a hard worker. Also at church, where he is a leader, he enjoys witnessing and working for the Lord and is sincere in what he does, generous, friendly . . . at times! What people don't know is that he has a violent temper if crossed, a harsh tongue. Things must go his way, otherwise . . . Mr Hyde comes out.'

Ann was concerned for him and prayed for him a great deal, especially in her once-daily waiting on the Lord. She scrutinized her own life — was she responsible for his character defect? She sought wisdom and guidance. Unchanged, he would surely miss heaven. She agonized for hours; and eventually felt blessed with an idea.

When Jim got home he was stunned to see the dining table prepared for a banquet. He clutched at his head. Had he forgotten her birthday . . . their anniversary? Apparently not. 'Something different, special,' she smiled. It was a feast, ending with his favourite, delicious, naughty-but-nice dessert. In a happy glow he pushed back his chair. 'Ann, sweetheart, there must be something behind all this.'

She put her arms round his neck and murmured, 'I'm blessed to have such a good husband. You are so faithful, putting home and me first. You love God and His truth. You're the hardest-working person I know. You're intelligent, sober. But . . . there is one thing that casts a shadow over my life. You can probably guess . . . .'

He knew, and frowned. 'Those times when . . . .' He fell silent.

'The temper flare-ups are not the real you. I'm sure they make you feel even more miserable than I feel.'

He slumped in his chair. 'I've tried so hard. You don't know how hard. It's a sin — the power of sin can be overwhelming . . . .'

After a while she said, 'I've an idea — from the Lord, I'm sure. It's this. Whenever there's a temper outburst, sit down and write out a cheque equivalent to one week's wages and give it to the church.'

He was appalled. 'We'd face bankruptcy!' But he promised to think about it.

Four weeks passed with no mention of the subject. Then he brought it up. 'Ann, the thing I've been mulling over. I appreciate your love, your concern for me. You're right. If any one thing is going to unfit me for heaven, that is it. Something must happen. You know, I pray three times a day. I've not had waiting-on-God times such as yours. No time, too much to do. Your cheque idea is drastic. How would it be if I forced myself to spend time daily waiting on God? Which would have the more powerful effect — the cheques, or the waiting on God?'

'Oh, the waiting on the Lord!' she exclaimed with the conviction of one who knew from personal experience.

They solemnly shook hands, then kissed.

Three months passed.

Jim saw the lighted candles on the dining table, and knew another banquet was in the offing.

She clung to him and said, 'You are a new man! Isn't it a miracle?'

'Never once,' he beamed. 'It was the Lord. I didn't do it. Do you know my secret? Mary, sitting at the feet of Jesus. I visualized that, emulated it. I sat at the feet of Jesus daily. My thinking changed. I feel liberated, free, with an inner joy I've never had before, a sense of release . . . a sense of salvation.' He stared into her misty eyes for what seemed like minutes. 'And it all started with my wife's waiting daily on God!'

---

[1]Hosea 14:2, KJV. [2]Matt. 11:28. [3]Ps. 27:14, KJV, emphasis ours. [4]Ps. 46:10, emphasis ours. [5]Ps. 62:1, 5, RAV. [6]Ps. 37:7. [7]Luke 6:12, RAV. [8]John 7:15. [9]Verse 46. [10]Luke 11:1.

How to baffle the enemy

Among the crowd of shoppers the girl, about 14 years of age, stood out because of her rapt expression. Intrigued, I smiled and she smiled back. 'What are you listening to?' I asked. She took the earphones from her ears, saying, 'Sorry, I didn't hear that.' This time she heard and said, 'It's a music cassette. Like to hear it?'

Because of her almost ecstatic expression my 'Please' was instantaneous. She held out the earphones. 'Oh,' I said, listening, my eyes on the little cassette player dangling from her shoulder.

'Isn't that something?' she asked eagerly.

I had a struggle. 'Well — rock music is not exactly my . . . passion. Do you listen to it often?'

'All the time! I've got all the big names, cassettes galore. I listen while dressing, having breakfast, walking to school — all day long. Even while having my bath. In fact,' she glowed, 'even while doing my homework!'

'Remarkable,' I responded. 'But while doing homework you obviously wouldn't be listening to the singer's words. Just the rhythm, if that is what you would call it.'

'No-o-o! The words are very important! I wouldn't miss one word, though I know them all by heart.'

'What a clever girl you must be, to concentrate at the same time on the music and the lyrics and your homework, and get good grades!'

'Oh, I don't get good grades,' she said cheerfully. 'But I get by. If I had to drop something I'd drop the school work. Rock music is my life.'

Somehow, I prefer the philosophy of a very great soul, the Apostle Paul. His words, 'To me, to live is Christ', have an immortal ring.[1]

While mountaineering I asked the leader, 'What do mountain climbing and rock-climbing mean to you?' He pondered deeply. 'This is my whole life,' he breathed. Some might say gardening is their life, or business, or pleasure, or travel, or a particular friendship. Paul could have said, 'Tent-making is my life', or 'Mission work is my life.' But to him there was only one focus: '*Christ is my life!*' 'It is a Person who fills my life, who gives meaning to it. He is my whole existence.'

He told the Colossian Christians that they were in possession of 'glorious riches' — nothing less than 'Christ in you, the hope of glory'.² One can imagine Paul's applying that to himself: 'Christ is in me, the hope of glory. Christ is not apart from me, but a part of me — the only glorious, heavenly part of me. Not for a moment are we separated. We have an unbroken bond — His life flowing into me; my gratitude, love and obedience flowing back. To me, to live is Christ and without Him there is no life.'

'Paul, I am a Christian,' I might have said, 'yet compared with you I seem to lack something. Please tell me your secret.'

I can hear Paul saying, 'The secret is in the mind, the thoughts. The Scriptures say, ''Above all else, guard your heart, for it is the wellspring of life.''³ What happens in your mind determines what you become. So let me tell you what you must fill your thoughts with: Whatever is true, whatever is noble, whatever is right, whatever is pure, whatever is lovely, whatever is admirable, excellent or praiseworthy.⁴ While I am making a tent — measuring, cutting, sewing — I'm thinking of truth, purity, heavenly things. Of course, my mind darts back repeatedly to the measurements and stitches. But even then I say, ''Quality work, to the honour of my Father in heaven.'' And I say, ''Thank You, Father, for these fingers, this cloth, this work.'' All through the day my thoughts tend *upward*.'

'Paul, how could you manage such control, such mind training?'

'As I said to the Philippians, ''I can do everything through him who gives me strength.''⁵ Jeremiah said the heart, or mind, is deceitful above all things. I don't rely on my intelligence, strength, resolve. I depend on Jesus my Lord, in me through the Holy Spirit. I plead for help in training my thoughts. And I receive the help.'

'So you live on a more dynamic level than ever?'

'No, I don't. I no longer live! I have been crucified with Christ. Christ now lives in me.[6] I'm not a better man. I'm a new creation by God.[7] I still have temptations, struggles as the fallen nature tries to assert itself. But by God's grace my entire life is set on an upward course.'

'My elder brother Paul ... how can I have this experience?'

'Pray continually. This I have urged.[8] Pray without ceasing. Don't pray three times a day as many do. Pray once only each day — all the time! If you feel you can't possibly, remember: "I can do everything through him who gives me the strength." '

There are three main kinds of prayers. Firstly, public prayer, as in family worship or on formal occasions; whenever two or more people pray together and one person utters the words while others listen and follow in their minds. Public prayer should be short and inclusive — 'we', not 'I'. It should be clearly audible, sincere and earnest, from the heart of one who has a genuine, fervent prayer life.

Secondly, private prayer, also referred to as secret or 'closet' prayer. This is the life of the soul. With scant private prayer the soul cannot flourish. It is secret because it is shared *only* with God. The soul is free from surrounding influences, free from excitement. Calmly yet fervently there is a reaching out to God. With quiet, simple faith we share our thoughts with God and open ourselves to His thoughts.

Thirdly, 'Pray continually.' We need to pray 'between prayers'. Unceasing prayer gives us an unbroken hold on our Father. Life from Him flows into us. From us there is a reaching out for God's will, to make it ours. We can do this while working, even while talking to someone. Our prayer thoughts flash to heaven and we remain tuned in to the Almighty.

This is marvellous protection. As one writer put it, 'These silent petitions rise like incense before the throne of grace; and the enemy is baffled.' As the Bible puts it, 'When the enemy shall come in like a flood, the Spirit of the Lord shall lift up a standard against him.'[9] The girl with her little cassette player had trained her mind to have rock music continuously. The Christian cannot afford not to do the same — with unceasing prayer!

A young man with an embarrassed air had come for counselling. 'Now you know my weakness,' he said after speaking for ten minutes. 'I can pray for an hour, gain the victory. Then I'll end my prayer and go out into the hurly-burly of life — and fall flat on my face!'

'Why do you stop praying?' I asked.

'How else? I've got to work.'

I gave him a text to read and he sat staring as though he had never seen it before — 1 Thessalonians 5:17. 'Surely that must be a figure of speech?'

Praying without cessation was one of the secrets in the life of Jesus. Paul acquired the art of praying continually, and to the Ephesians used the words 'keep on praying'. You can learn to obey that rule.

'If I could do that,' he murmured, 'I'd never fall into sin. Obviously, you can't sin and pray at the same time.'

'Do you want some suggestions on how to train the mind in unceasing prayer? You do? Good, here they are.

'Point one — in your prayers plead with the Lord to enable you prayerfully to keep in touch between your prayer sessions.

'Point two — select a text for each day and keep it on a card where you can see it. Turn it over in your mind. Thank God for it and make it part of your continual prayers.

'Point three — train your mind so that everything you see or hear or touch will remind you of the Creator.

'Point four — memorize hymns and hum them to yourself or sing them.

'Point five — talk to others about God; His character, His Word, His providences. Don't preach at people or bore them. Be brief, interesting, simple and enthusiastic.

'Of course, if you like, you can take a leaf out of the book of the rock-music girl — you can carry a personal cassette player about, with religious music cassettes. Like Enoch, you can walk with God. Enoch was able to have this uninterrupted walk with God because of his prayer-life. Constant prayer will help you to do the same.'

The young man struggled, suffered defeats. He came to understand himself better. He knew Satan was working hard to obstruct the way to God's throne for him, with efforts to preoccupy his mind. But as he wrestled on, his successes increased. In the end, in addition to closet praying, he was maintaining a constant communication with God.

'It's my lifeline!' he exulted. 'I'm hanging on to that lifeline. If I let go I'll drift away. So I never stop praying. You won't believe this, but . . . my entire conscious life is a prayer. I'd never have thought it possible. How did I ever exist without this sublime experience? Continual prayer has turned me into an overcomer over my sin! ''Amazing grace! how sweet the sound that saved a wretch like me. I once was lost, but now am found; was blind, but now I see.'' '

---

[1]Phil. 1:21. [2]Col. 1:27. [3]Prov. 4:23. [4]Phil. 4:8. [5]Verse 13. [6]Gal. 2:20. [7]2 Cor. 5:17. [8]1 Thess. 5:17. [9]Isa. 59:19, KJV.

Prayer for others

'I've prayed and prayed for my daughter to become a Christian. My prayers have never been answered!' said a worried mother. God could have forced the girl to believe, like a programmed robot — but He has given every human a free will, and respects it.

Does this mean that intercessory prayers are futile? Not at all, as we shall see.

'I've been praying for my brother Larry in Australia,' said Penelope. 'I love him and want to see him converted. But doesn't the Lord also want him converted? Of course! Doesn't God love him much, much more than I do? After all, Jesus died to save him! The Holy Spirit is already drawing my brother in love. Do my prayers persuade God to put more effort into it? The implications of that thought are terrible! God is absolute love, so He must already be doing everything, short of using force, for Larry . . . for every soul on earth. Then why all my huff and puff and strain of praying, when it does not add one iota to the exertions of heaven on Larry's behalf?'

God does indeed love every soul on earth. Jesus died for everyone. God is concerned for Larry and wants to send someone to labour with him; but He still commands, 'Pray that I will send a labourer.' Matthew's plea was: 'Pray ye therefore the Lord of the harvest, that he will send forth labourers into his harvest.'[1] The harvest field of humanity belongs to God. He wants to send help with the harvesting. But He urges, 'Pray that I may send help.' Why?

We should especially like to know the philosophy behind prayer for others when we see how the great Apostle Paul relied on it. 'Brothers, pray for us,' he begged,[2] obviously convinced that it does make a difference. He takes the matter even further: 'I urge, then, first of all, that requests, prayers, intercession and thanksgiving be made for everyone.'[3] How encouraging. We can pray for family members, friends, people in authority whose decisions affect many lives. We can even pray for our enemies![4] Moreover, we can pray with 'thanksgiving'. It is as though we are saying, 'Thank you, Lord, for what You are going to do for them.'[5] Paul was sure that prayer for others was not in vain.

Why humans praying for humans is part of God's plan can be better understood when the following is kept in mind.

God rules by love, not compulsion. Ages ago an angel close to the throne took advantage of the freedom God allows by toying with wrong thoughts.[6] At first he was probably surprised at himself, and recoiled. But he returned to the exciting, dangerous excursions; and the more he daydreamed the more fascinated he became. At last he started insinuating things against his Maker's character, dropping ideas into other angelic minds. God was supposed to be unfair, demanding too much of His creatures, too fond of adulation; behind a mask of love was a tyrant.

The Creator gave him every chance to draw back and save himself, but sin indulged has bewitching power.[7] He became bolder. Eventually there was war in heaven between God and the accuser, and their followers.[8] The rebels were cast out of heaven,[9] and enticed Adam into joining them. Thereby they won a foothold on planet Earth.[10]

The great controversy between God and Satan goes on.[11] True to His fair, loving nature, God is allowing Satan to work out his government on earth. This soon became a demonstration to all intelligent beings throughout the universe of the suffering and disaster that his ideas inevitably spawn. God is seen as a Being of love, gentleness and patient persuasion, taking on Himself the guilt of humans[12] and paying the price so that men can escape death. Satan and his angels are seen as those who deceive,[13] resulting in suffering and death. The clash of ideas has turned the world into a vast, perpetual battlefield.

And the winner? Satan is mortal, finite. God is immortal, infinite in power and wisdom, incomparable.[14] Satan's defeat was sealed at Calvary.[15] Yet Satan has such a vast majority of humans as his followers that the Bible calls him 'the god of this world'.[16] This will only change at the second coming of Christ the Lord.

Meanwhile the controversy rages. The Creator could in an

instant obliterate Satan and all his hosts. But then in the endless ages ahead the thought could arise that God had unfairly
used His omnipotence against puny created beings . . .
wasn't He tyrannical after all?

To make eternity safe for angels and humans, without one
discordant note ever again among the vast galaxies, God
limits Himself, forcing nothing. So powerful are His blessing
and presence that in their full glory no man, woman or child
could resist the urge to do homage.[17] Consequently God
limits Himself severely in His dealings with humans; and at
the same time also restricts Satan so that his power and cun-
ning will not be irresistible to any God-seeking soul.

God's character is the issue in the great cosmic war; the
Enemy of souls tries to make sure that God's actions are misunderstood. Even fine, noble, honourable things can be
misunderstood; let alone things which are ambiguous or
incompletely described — as with much in the Bible. But
God's love longs that every person will be saved.[18] To this end
He provides clear opportunities for discovery and faith, so
that no person of sound mind has any excuse for missing
eternal life.[19] Yet God is willing to do even more. Where a
person feels a need for divine strength, angels are instructed
to impart grace and power *if requested*. A prayer interceding
for that person could provide the extra help at a vital moment. No wonder Paul was so eager to be remembered in
others' prayers!

Of course, our heavenly Father constantly gives many good
things whether asked or not — beating hearts, thinking
minds, sunshine, rain, the Bible, guardian angels. But other
blessings, such as the Holy Spirit in abundance, He gives
only when prayed for.[20] Satan watched vainly for evidence
that God is unfairly doing too much. When intercessory
prayer is followed by God's doing more, He can say, 'I have
been asked by a subject of my kingdom.'

That Christian mother's prayers for her unbelieving daughter's conversion brought additional angel ministry to her
daughter's side. Of course, they had no mandate to coerce;
but the witness of God's love was intensified. Twenty months
after the mother's death the daughter, haunted by the thought

of her mother's tender, persistent prayers, surrendered to Christ.

Prayer for others is therefore a power for good. It blesses the one who is the object of prayer, and makes the one who prays a co-worker with God.[21]

Pray for those for whom you have a burden, preferably at a set time every day. At times share this intercessory prayer experience with others — at a prayer meeting, or with one or two fellow believers at home. Pray that the Holy Spirit will work powerfully with the one concerned. If possible, keep in close touch with him or her, by letter if nothing else. Show love, sympathy and kindness. Let the person know of your prayers, and even the time of day when they are offered.

Jesus is the great supplicant on behalf of others.[22] When we pray for others we are joining Him in this holy work. He will add His intercession to our prayers, and claim for the sinner the gift of the Holy Spirit's special ministry.

'Pray for each other' we are urged.[23] Because prayer is directed to the Almighty and taken seriously by Him, it is the greatest force available to the faith-rich child of God.

---

[1]Matt. 9:38, KJV. [2]1 Thess. 5:25. [3]1 Tim. 2:1. [4]Matt. 5:44. [5]1 Tim. 2:1-5, see The Living Bible. [6]Isa. 14:12-14; Ezek. 28:11-17. [7]Heb. 3:13. [8]Rev. 12:7-9. [9]Luke 10:18. [10]Gen. 3. [11]Rev. 12:12-17. [12]Rom. 5:6-10. [13]Rev. 13:14; 12:9; Matt. 24:24. [14]Isa. 46:5. [15]John 3:14, 15. [16]2 Cor. 4:4, KJV. [17]Isa. 6:5. [18]1 Tim. 2:4. [19]Rom. 1:18-21. [20]Luke 11:13. [21]2 Cor. 6:1. [22]Isa. 53:12. [23]James 5:16.

Every good and perfect gift

What state of mind do the following three episodes in the life of Christ have in common?

• Like the other guests, Jesus is reclining at the table laden with food. The woman comes up behind Him, weeping silently. Tears drop on His feet and she wipes them off with her hair, kissing His feet and pouring perfume on them.

The host's lip curls in scorn at the thought, 'If He were a prophet, He'd know her and her sinful soul and not allow her to touch Him.'

Jesus said, 'Simon, a word in your ear. Two men owe money to a money-lender — one 500 denarii, the other 50. Neither could settle, so he cancelled both debts. Which of the two will love him the more?'

'The one with the bigger debt,' said Simon.

'Yes. Do you see this girl? I came into your house and you provided no water for my feet, but she splashed her tears on my feet and dried them with her hair. You gave me no kiss, but she has hardly stopped kissing my feet. You put no common oil on my head, but she poured perfumed oil on my feet. So I tell you, her many sins have been forgiven . . . you see the evidence, her great love.'

• The lepers kept their distance, as the law required; but they shouted, 'Jesus, Master, have pity on us.'

To give faith a chance to come into play over the next few days, Jesus said: 'Go and show yourselves to the priests.'

Considering their options, they decided to obey, and every day as they made their way towards distant Jerusalem found the leprosy still with them. Then one morning as they saw Jerusalem's skyline they burst into shouts of exuberant joy as they found all traces of the leprosy gone.

Nine went home to resume a normal life. One, despised by the Jews because he was a Samaritan, walked the length of Judea and flung himself at Jesus' feet in gratitude.

• A man was brought before Jesus. Deaf from birth, his

desperate attempts to speak had resulted in strange grunts that here and there resembled words. He looked bewildered, not knowing what to make of Jesus. Jesus led him away from witnesses who would too easily attach magical meanings to the unusual procedure which He was about to follow.

Putting a finger in each deaf ear, Jesus gave him a look so encouraging that the man's face lit up with hope. Jesus touched His own tongue, then the man's, to convey the message, 'Your tongue will speak like mine.' Then he glanced up to direct the man's thoughts to God and heaven.

'Be opened!' He ordered the deaf ears.

The man could suddenly hear and speak. 'Don't talk about your healing,' Jesus said. But nothing could stop the words of thanks and praise pouring from him as he rushed back to the crowd.

Praise and thanksgiving distinguish each event. And very properly so — marvellous gifts had been received. Forgiveness of sins and freedom from guilt; the removal of a deadly disease wreaking havoc with the body; and silence replaced by sound, the gift of sharing thoughts and words.

But where . . . where were the nine Jewish lepers? Those who never felt a decent need to say, 'Wonderful! Thank You!'?

Gratitude is the very least we can offer God. 'Do not be anxious about anything, but in everything, by prayer and petition, *with thanksgiving*, present your requests to God.'[1] 'Pray continually; *give thanks in all circumstances*, for this is God's will for you in Christ Jesus.'[2]

Give thanks in *all* circumstances? What if the circumstances are unpleasant, even agonizing?

Those ten lepers approaching Jesus were not devoid of gifts or blessings. In the first place they had life. 'Anyone who is among the living has hope — even a live dog is better off than a dead lion! . . . the dead know nothing.'[3] Second, they could hear and talk. Third, they had the energy and ability to walk across Judea to Jerusalem. Fourth, they had access to food and water and clothing. Fifth — they could utter a prayer to Jesus. The story could go on — the beauty of flowers, a rivulet on a hillside, sunrise and sunset, a rainbow, birds, warming rays of the sun . . . but the grand, exalted privilege of communion with the Father of the universe is the supreme gift.

Memorable also is the experience of Paul and Silas. Paul was troubled over the plight of a demon-possessed girl and addressed the demon, ' "In the name of Jesus Christ I command you to come out of her!" '[4] At once the girl was well and normal.

For this Paul and Silas were seized, accused of inciting an uproar, set upon by the maddened crowd, stripped, beaten, severely flogged, thrown into prison and locked into stocks.

Paul was the man who told the Thessalonians to 'give thanks in all circumstances.'[5] When his circumstances soured and he was bloody and in excruciating pain, did he remember his own injunction?

'About midnight Paul and Silas were praying and singing hymns to God . . . .'[6] They must have been saying, 'Lord, we could have been dead at the hands of the mob — but we're alive! Thank You for our preservation. We could have been maimed for life — we're not. We could have been suffering for a bad deed. How blessed we are that we can suffer for a good deed! Thank You that in some small measure we can share in the sufferings of our Lord.'

Their songs of joyous, thankful praise resounded through the prison.

Those 'with eyes to see' will have a plethora of reasons to be grateful and to direct their thanks and praise to God. God is incessantly at work in our lives, to save; His angels befriend us; we have the Bible; and the Holy Spirit within is not 'a spirit of timidity, but a spirit of power, of love'.[7]

'Praise the Lord, O my soul; all my inmost being, praise his holy name. Praise the Lord, O my soul, and forget not all his benefits.'[8] He forgives, removes guilt.[9] He has preserved our life.[10] 'The Lord is compassionate and gracious, slow to anger, abounding in love.'[11] God does not treat us as we deserve — we deserve death, not grace.[12] His love for us is incomprehensible.[13] He knows us completely.[14]

'The Lord has established his throne in heaven, and his

kingdom rules over all. Praise the Lord, you his angels, you mighty ones who do his bidding, who obey his word. Praise the Lord, all his heavenly hosts, you his servants who do his will. Praise the Lord, all his works everywhere in his dominion. Praise the Lord, O my soul.'[15]

A perceptive heart will be grateful, and a grateful heart will overflow in thanks and praise.

> The other day upon a bus
> I saw a girl with golden hair.
> I envied her — she looked so gay —
> And wished I were as fair.
> Then suddenly she rose to leave;
> I watched her hobble down the aisle.
> She had but one leg, bore a crutch . . .
> And as she passed she smiled!
>
> O God, forgive me when I whine —
> I have two legs, the world is mine!
>
> Later I paused to buy some sweets.
> The lad who sold them had such charm
> I stayed to talk to him a while —
> If I were late 'twould do no harm.
> Then as I turned to leave he said
> 'Thank you, you've been so kind,
> I like to talk to folk like you —
> You see, I'm blind.'
>
> O God, forgive me when I whine.
> I have two eyes, the world is mine!
> — Author Unknown

'Every good and perfect gift is from above, coming down from the Father of the heavenly lights.'[16]

True prayer will always include thanksgiving and praise. If the loving-kindness of God elicited more thanksgiving and praise, we would have far more power in prayer.

---

[1] Phil. 4:6, emphasis ours. [2] 1 Thess. 5:17, 18, emphasis ours. [3] Eccles. 9:4, 5. [4] Acts 16:18. [5] 1 Thess. 5:18. [6] Acts 16:25. [7] 2 Tim. 1:7. [8] Ps. 103:1, 2. [9] Verses 3, 12. [10] Verses 3, 4. [11] Verse 8. [12] Verse 10. [13] Verses 11, 17. [14] Verse 14. [15] Verses 19-22. [16] James 1:17.

Blank cheque texts examined

In ways weird and wonderful — and sometimes hard to detect — the Bible has often been distorted, its true meaning missed.

Sometimes a text hits us in the face with the need to dig deeper. ' "If anyone comes to me and does not hate his father and mother, . . . he cannot be my disciple." '[1] What, hate my parents in order to be a Christian, when God's Word commands me to ' "Honour your father and your mother" '?[2] No, the meaning that springs to the mind of the modern reader is not the true one. Going deeper one discovers that the Hebrew hyperbolic idiom, taken into the Greek, means 'to love less' — our love for God must be supreme. The parallel passage in Matthew removes all uncertainty: ' "Anyone who loves his father or mother more than me is not worthy of me." '[3]

In Matthew we are given an apparently sweeping promise: ' "Ask and it will be given to you; seek and you will find; knock and the door will be opened to you. For anyone who asks receives; he who seeks finds; and to him who knocks, the door will be opened." '[4] If I pray to be a millionaire, will the result be guaranteed? Or if John prays that Jennifer will fall in love with and marry him, will he find her indifference replaced by infatuation?

It is a noble and necessary thing to pray that the Holy Spirit will guide us in a true understanding of God's Word, including His promises. The first thing we will want to know is, 'What did this passage mean to the writer and his readers?' The second is, 'What does it mean today?' No matter which Bible passage is being scrutinized, the following will help.

• A sincere desire to learn and understand, with a view to fuller obedience. Earnestness will help us not to begrudge the time and prayerful effort needed.

• Good translations. Only experts in the original Hebrew, Aramaic and Greek can dispense with these. Translation is an art, not a science. Since much of language is made up of idioms, mechanical word-for-word translation is impossible. The translator must do his utmost to plumb the meaning in one language, then as closely as possible reproduce it in the second. Some translations are intended to present the original as literally as possible — the King James Version and the Revised Standard Version are examples. Others concentrate on intended meaning; The Living Bible helpfully translates Luke 14:26: ' "Anyone who wants to be my follower must love me far more than he does his own father, mother . . . ." ' — ignoring the word 'hate' in the original Greek. Other translations, like the New International Version, fall somewhere between the literal and 'dynamic' methods. All translations have certain limitations — particularly a translation made by one denomination, which could hardly escape suspicion of favouring its own teachings. Hence the imperative need to compare translations.

• A good Bible dictionary and good commentaries can sometimes help with background history, problems of language and cultural aspects that can be determinative.

Wishing to understand our verses in Matthew, ' "Ask and it will be given you . . . " ', in a sound and balanced way, uninfluenced by wishful thinking, we shall give due weight to *four* contexts.

First, the *context of prayer*. 'Lord, I don't want to interpret this according to my desires, my will, my hopes, or others' ideas. Please lead me to see it as You see it! At all costs I must have the truth on this. Bring my mind into harmony with Yours!'

Second, the *immediate context* of the passage. In the New Testament, Matthew, Mark, Luke and John consist of short narrative stories and short teaching passages. The immediate context is that story or passage. The book of Acts is an extended narrative, the immediate context being the incident described. In the Epistles the immediate context is the paragraph. In Revelation it is generally the vision.

Third is *the context of the whole book*. The words, ' "The righteous will live by faith" '[5] are nicely balanced by 'Do we,

then, nullify the law by this faith? Not at all! Rather, we
uphold the law.'[6]

Finally, the witness on that subject of *the whole Bible*. We
have already seen that living by faith in Christ does not
relieve us of the obligation to obey God's moral law — the
Ten Commandments. In Matthew 5:17-19 the Lord carries this
further. ' "Do not think that I have come to abolish the Law or
the Prophets; I have not come to abolish them but to fulfil
them. I tell you the truth, until heaven and earth disappear,
not the smallest letter, not the least stroke of a pen, will by
any means disappear from the Law until everything is accomplished. Anyone who breaks one of the least of these
commandments and teaches others to do the same will be
called least in the kingdom of heaven, but whoever practises
and teaches these commands will be called great in the kingdom of heaven." ' This is echoed in Luke 16:17 and Isaiah
8:20. The context of the entire Bible is therefore pivotal.

What the Scripture means today cannot be at total variance
with what it meant when first given. The human heart is the
same, sin is the same, the Ten Commandments are the same,
and only grace could *ever* save from sin, disobedience and
death. The Holy Spirit still speaks, offers an eternal hope,
and illumines the sacred pages for us. Helped by a grasp of
the historical meaning of a specific passage, we can more se-
curely find the meaning for us today.

Let us examine Matthew 7:7, 8. Read in isolation it does
look like a blank cheque. Just ask, and you will receive!
Millionaireship or the love of Jennifer — why not? But the
context can never safely be ignored.

What is the immediate connection? The promise of
Matthew 7 is part of the Sermon on the Mount.[7] This sermon
deals with Christ's kingdom of grace which He has established on this planet of rebellion. Those who join it must be
exceptional people. They must in the first place be men and
women of the highest ideals. Secondly, they must plan and
live for the kingdom of heaven. The following examples
reveal their spirit.

- Shun anger, or you will be regarded as a murderer.[8]

- Pure thoughts only — lustful thoughts render you an adulterer.[9]
  - Honesty, integrity and sincerity must mark your life.[10]
  - No revenge: 'turn the other cheek.'[11]
  - Love your enemies.[12]
  - All your motives must be noble and true.[13]
  - Shun materialism.[14]
  - Put all your trust in God and live by faith.[15]
- 'Judge not' others' motives; avoid the habit of censorious, sharp and usually unjust criticism.[16]

Do all the above exactly describe you? It is not easy to love your enemies, turn the other cheek, be noble and pure-minded, live by faith, shun anger and 'judge not'. Where shall we go for help? To God. '"Ask and it will be given to you; seek and you will find; knock and the door will be opened to you."'

We pondered earlier, 'If I pray to be a millionaire, will the result be guaranteed? Or if John prays that Jennifer will fall in love with and marry him, will he find her indifference replaced by infatuation?' The context answers the questions. The Lord Jesus was talking about the spiritual characteristics that should mark His followers!

Some Christians will frown unhappily and say, 'I can see the context and how the prayer phrase fits in. But I want a nice house, a new car, health and a Mediterranean holiday. I'm going to pray, "Lord, You said ask and I'd receive, so I'm asking for a house, a car, health and so on." What's wrong with that?'

I may try to hold someone to a promise he never made, and insist that I prefer to interpret his words according to my wishes — but that hardly qualifies me for point number three above! The true follower of Jesus Christ will not try to manipulate the Almighty; he will approach Him with reverence, seeking to honour Him in everything.

How heartening it is, when faced with points 1 to 9 above, to remember that the Lord has given the explicit assurances of Matthew 7:7, 8 to *all* who pray, seeking sanctification diligently and perseveringly, their eye single to the glory of God. The Lord will help. His love is with you. His 'giving' promise is yours.

Another Scripture often quoted is in Mark: ' "Whatever you ask for in prayer, believe that you have received it, and it will be yours." '[17]

The immediate context is the miracle of the drying up of the fig tree, Christ's acted parable. On Monday morning of the crucifixion week Christ spotted the tree, so luxuriantly leafed out that one could not but expect to find fruit on it. There was none, and He said, ' "May no one ever eat fruit from you again." '[18]

The next morning His disciples exclaimed, 'Rabbi, look! The fig tree you cursed yesterday is dead from the roots up!'[19]

They were stunned with a conviction of Christ's divine power. A tree can't hear, understand, obey. A fig tree can't within twenty-four hours be as dried out as a mummy! With just a word this had happened. God's awesome power was in this miracle.

Jesus could have replied, 'The fig tree represents the nation of Israel. The luxuriant leaves symbolize their religiosity — all ceremonies and offerings and tradition and show. The lack of fruit shows their superficiality; no heart religion. And the drying up, their rejection as My Father's chosen people.'

That would have been both true and within the immediate context. But they were not ready for this revelation. Further, they had a pressing need. In three days they would see their Master hanging on the cross, His work apparently brought to nothing. Their greatest need then would be faith — a faith that would hold on to the miracle that they had just found so sensational, so eloquent with Christ's divinity. They needed a faith to live by when all seemed dark and lost.

And so Jesus spoke these challenging words to them: ' "Have faith in God. . . . I tell you the truth, if anyone says to this mountain, *(Mount of Olives, on whose slope they were standing; figuratively, mountains of difficulty, such as seeing their Lord arrested, scourged and killed, and they desperately needed some glimmer of understanding and hope)*, 'Go, throw yourself into the sea', and does not doubt in his heart but believes that what he says will happen, it will be done for him. Therefore I tell you, *whatever you ask for in prayer (for instance, 'Father, help me to hold on to the divinity of my Master! Help me to understand why He had to give Himself up to die! Help me to recall any instruction He might have given in the past to prepare us for His coming death — words we probably failed to take to heart! Help me not to despair, not to abandon hope, to stand in courage — uncomprehending strength, if need be. May that manifestation of divine power in the drying up of the fig tree three days ago stabilize my spirit, my faith'),* believe that you have received it, and it will be yours." '[20]

How they needed those words! Within hours what faith they had would be put to the supreme test . . . and found wanting. A crisis was upon them. The Lord was promising them strength and understanding. Not one of them needed to betray Christ.

What does Mark 11:24 convey to us today?

Firstly, *the need of faith.* Faith in God: His power, wisdom and love. Faith is trusting God — believing that He loves us and knows what is best for our good. Thus faith leads us to choose not our way and desires, but God's way and will. Faith acknowledges that we belong to God and not to ourselves.

Secondly, the assurance *that in Christ every deficiency of our character may be supplied,* every sin forgiven, every fault corrected and every excellence developed.

'But these are all spiritual things,' someone may say. 'I am interested in my temporal needs. How can faith help me temporally?'

Faith says, 'I believe in God. He *is.* I believe nothing is beyond His power, knowledge or wisdom. He knows my temporal needs. He cares. He will answer my temporal prayers if He, knowing the end from the beginning, should see that this is the highest good for me. If possessions would be a disservice to me in the long run, He will not give them. I'll keep my temporal needs, like my spiritual ones, before God — with a "Your will be done!" I trust God with my life and all my needs.'

Faith is not feeling. Faith is the product of a partnership with the Holy Spirit. It is a faculty invested with power. We choose to exercise faith at all times. When the sun is shining and our thoughts are buoyant, yes; but faith really comes into its own when an impenetrable gloom shuts us in, as happened to the disciples after the death of their Master. The very time to exercise faith is when we feel depressed because of our own unmeritorious life or forbidding circumstances, when we feel destitute of the Holy Spirit. True faith rests on God's goodness — His kindness, tender love, forgiving spirit. It also rests on God's promises, such as: ' ''Come to me, all you who are weary and burdened, and I will give you rest. Take my yoke upon you and learn from me, for I am gentle and humble in heart, and you will find rest for your souls. For my yoke is easy and my burden is light.'' '[21]

We can say, 'Lord, You know my burdens, so grievous that I feel squashed by them. Thank You for Your invitation to come, for Your promise of a rest pervading my inner being. Here I am, dear Father! Please be my Helper, my refuge! Please forgive my sins of neglect . . . my sins of transgression . . . . And now, Father, by faith I claim Your promise of peace. Thank You for flooding me with this peace!'

Here is faith, naked faith, to believe that we have received the blessing even before we realize it. Then feeling follows! We feel uplifted, energized by the Holy Spirit. We have claimed God's explicit promise of restfulness and peace, and experienced Mark's statement: ' ''Believe that you have received it, and it will be yours.'' '[22] Faith is ours to exercise; the joyful feeling and blessing are God's to give.

So we see that faith is not a magic charm. Faith is not rubbing the lamp and the genie appears. It is not an instrument to use to get the gods of superstition — or even the unique Creator — to give us all we long for. Rather is it a divinely supplied power that changes us, lifts us above selfish perspectives and shortsighted priorities, and brings our thinking into harmony with our heavenly Father's.

That is peace, 'the peace of God, which transcends all understanding.'[23] 'Your life is now hidden with Christ in God.'[24]

All God's promises are conditional. They are conditional

even if the condition is not stated in the immediate context.

'I will do whatever you ask in my name,' sounds very easy. *Whatever* — surely that sounds unrestricted, licence to choose whatever takes your fancy. The only qualification seems to be 'in my name', which is merely fitting in three words and waiting for heaven to deliver what we have ordered!

This passage is found in the gospel of John: ' "And I will do whatever you ask in my name, so that the Son may bring glory to the Father. You may ask me for anything in my name, and I will do it." '[25]

Jesus spoke these words to His disciples on the evening before His crucifixion. As part of the same discourse He said, ' "If you remain in me and my words remain in you, ask whatever you wish, and it will be given you." '[26]

Three conditions are given. We must pray in the name of Jesus Christ; we must remain in Him; and His 'words' or teachings must remain in us. ' "Remain in me, and I will remain in you," ' the Lord says.[27]

It is hard to think of a more intimate relationship than for Christ to live *in* you, while you live *in* Him. His life is in you; His truths, principles and spirit make you distinctive. Because of your harmony with God, your main desire is to discover His will and co-operate with it. In your prayers you will ask for those things that our Father has commanded or promised. Examples are: forgiveness of sin;[28] the Holy Spirit dominant within;[29] in doctrine, the full truth of the Bible pursued and embraced;[30] an inner peace that triumphs over 'the slings and arrows of outrageous fortune', even 'a sea of troubles' in Shakespearean terms;[31] strength to keep God's moral law;[32] self-control;[33] wisdom to speak for and rightly represent your heavenly Father.[34]

You will also pray for the necessities of this life — things like shelter, food, a knowledge of wise living to promote physical and mental health, health itself, safety, wisdom in the management of money, friendships, education — submitting these requests to the will of God. Your priorities in prayer will show that you are indeed living in Christ and He in you. And living in Him you will pray according to His purposes, depend upon His grace, and do His work. Your prayers, directed and moulded by the Holy Spirit, will most certainly be answered. 'I will do whatever you ask in my name, so that the Son may bring glory to the Father.'

In times of severe illness the minds of believers tend to gravitate towards James 5:15, 16: 'The prayer offered in faith will make the sick person well; the Lord will raise him up. If he has sinned, he will be forgiven. Therefore confess your sins to each other and pray for each other so that you may be healed. The prayer of a righteous man is powerful and effective.'

To repeat: all promises are conditional. One condition leaps out of the passage itself — confession of sin, 'so that you may be healed'. Lack of contrition and confession would be an impediment; the same would apply to wrong motives. 'You ask with wrong motives.'[35] Is the motive unselfish? Is it to bring glory to God? Further insight comes from the words 'confess . . . to each other'.[36] Why 'each other'? 'What causes fights and quarrels among you?'[37] This gives one serious pause. Squabbling hardly goes with prayers that God can honour. Surely, if these believers wanted their prayers heard they had to stop fighting and quarrelling among themselves! Another vignette: 'You do not have, because you do not ask God'[38] — so prayer was in short supply among them. When they did pray, they inclined to selfish motives.[39] They also revealed a tendency to worldliness.[40] 'Wash your hands, you sinners, and purify your hearts, you who are double-minded.'[41]

No wonder James exhorts, 'Submit yourselves, then, to God.'[42] Submission would require a single-minded trust in God; and trust in God excludes prescribing to God what He should or should not do. The true believer will not make demands or insist. His attitude will be: 'Lord, please heal, on the basis of Christ's merits, if healing would best glorify Your name. Your will be done.'

This harmonizes with the Holy Spirit's words through John. 'If we ask anything *according to his will*, he hears us.'[43]

James's message is: 'Clear away all obstructions. Then pray

in faith. God *can* heal. God is love, so His *wish* is to heal. Don't be double-minded, asking for healing yet convinced that God won't do it. Have absolute confidence in God, *and* submit yourselves to Him and His will. If your request harmonizes with God's decision, which has the best possible outcome in view, ''the Lord will raise him up''.'

Not to 'submit yourselves to God' can have disastrous effects. Albert asked me to hold an anointing service according to James 5 for his cancer-ridden son-in-law. I did so, qualifying my request for healing with the wish that God's will be done. Their response to the submissive words was less than fervent.

No miracle ensued and Albert had a minister flown in to repeat the anointing service. The patient's condition deteriorated markedly after this. Albert decided to take over spiritual ministrations. Laying hands on the sufferer he prayed, 'Lord, You promised. We have had the anointing. You said if we believed You would raise up the one who is sick. I believe, believe utterly. I claim Your promise. According to Your word I believe that You *will* raise up Arthur! Thank You, Lord! I know You have touched him, the cancer is conquered! Glory to Your name!'

Later he told me, 'God cannot lie. So the fault must lie with me. I thought I was a true child of God. I was mistaken. I must fast; God must show me the idols in my heart. I must wrestle with God in prayer. I must be changed, then the Holy Spirit will work in me and Arthur will rise like the paralytic of Bethesda.'

Not long after Arthur's funeral Albert was confined to a hospital for the mentally ill, where he later died.

When believers 'submit themselves to God', even 'humble themselves before the Lord', the assurance is given 'and He will lift you up'.[44] They may go on praying in earnest faith, but at the same time they will have peace of mind. God is in control; He makes the good, wise, compassionate decisions. The divine gift of peace will lift and carry the supplicants.

> I said: 'Let me walk in the fields.'
> He said: 'No, walk in the town.'
> I said: 'There are no flowers there.'

He said: 'No flowers, but a crown.'

I said: 'But the air is thick,
And fogs are veiling the sun.'
He answered: 'Yet souls are sick,
And souls in the dark undone . . . .'

I cast one look at the fields,
Then set my face to the town;
He said: 'My child, do you yield?
Will you leave the flowers for the crown?'

Then into His hand went mine;
And into my heart came He;
And I walk in a light divine,
The path I had feared to see.
— *George MacDonald*

I shall continue to place my needs before my heavenly Father. But instead of expecting 'blank cheques' from Him I shall offer God the blank cheque of my faith in His will for me — whatever it may be.

---

[1]Luke 14:26. [2]Exod. 20:12. [3]Matt. 10:37. [4]Matt. 7:7, 8. [5]Rom. 1:17. [6]Rom. 3:31, emphasis ours. [7]Matthew chapters 5-7. [8]5:21-26. [9]Verses 27-32. [10]Verses 33-37. [11]Verses 38-42. [12]Verses 43-48. [13]6:1-18. [14]Verses 19-23. [15]Verses 24-34. [16]7:1-6. [17]Mark 11:24. [18]Verse 14. [19]See verse 21. [20]Verses 22-24, emphasis ours. [21]Matt. 11:28-30. [22]Mark 11:24. [23]Phil. 4:7. [24]Col. 3:3. [25]John 14:13, 14. [26]John 15:7. [27]Verse 4. [28]1 John 1:9. [29]Luke 11:13; 1 Cor. 2:13. [30]John 16:13. [31]Matt. 11:28, 29; John 14:27. [32]1 Sam. 15:22; 1 Cor. 7:19; Rev. 14:12. [33]Rom. 13:14; Gal. 5:22. [34]Matt. 28:19, 20; 10:19. [35]James 4:3. [36]James 5:16. [37]James 4:1. [38]Verse 2. [39]Verse 3. [40]Verse 4. [41]Verse 8. [42]Verse 7, emphasis ours. [43]1 John 5:14, emphasis ours. [44]James 4:7, 10.

'Watch unto prayer'

The life of Nehemiah offers valuable lessons in prayer. He was a trusted official in the court of Artaxerxes I, King of Persia, in the capital Susa, when news reached him in 445 BC that Jerusalem's city wall had been broken down and the gates burned. This plunged him into mourning and fasting; but he had to keep up an appearance of cheerfulness — Persia's kings were quick to spot moods and suspect plots on their lives. One day a moment of unguarded sadness caused the mask to slip.

'What's troubling you?' the King demanded.

This was a crisis. One word or even a fleeting expression could seal Nehemiah's doom. For four months he had been pouring out his heart in prayer that the King might be moved to help God's people in Jerusalem. Now, flashing a silent prayer for guidance to God, he spoke. 'Your Majesty, my ancestral city lies exposed and vulnerable to enemies, its walls broken and gates gutted. Is this not cause for tears?'

The King considered him carefully. 'Do you have a request to put before me?'

Nehemiah knew this was the make-or-break moment as he silently appealed for wisdom and divine intervention. Then his words came, tactful, balanced, sincere. The King was impressed.

'All right,' he said. 'I'll do what you ask. I'll release you from your duties here for a time, and give you letters of authority. You'll be able to draw on the royal treasury to finance the undertaking.'

Four months of fervent prayer, and now crisis guidance . . . . Nehemiah was overwhelmed with gratitude.

He could have become impulsive or overconfident; instead he entered into meticulous planning. While putting his entire trust in God, he set to work as though everything depended on him. He was alert to Satan's opposition. Enemies could be moved upon to attack his caravan on the way to Jerusalem. Prudently he begged the King for a military escort and was granted one.

Arriving at Jerusalem, Nehemiah said not a word about his mission. Information might stir enemies to violence. He was taking no chances.

The wall and gates had to be inspected. Nehemiah waited one night till the city was asleep, and after midnight set out to make the survey by moonlight. Then he spent the rest of the night in prayer.

In the morning he called all the leaders together. He could have thought, 'God and the King are behind my plans, so I'll just lay all the facts on the table and in the King's name command co-operation.'

Instead he set to work with exquisite tact to win their confidence and sympathy and generate enthusiasm. Even now he did not divulge the fact of his midnight circuit of the walls — someone was bound to take offence on a point of procedure. He sketched the reproach God's name and religion suffered among heathen nations because of Jerusalem's decay, appealed to their nobler instincts . . . and won their zealous support.

When the work started, the enemies got busy. They tried psychological warfare: 'Nehemiah, we hear you are a traitor to the King, secretly plotting independence.' Nehemiah denied all charges and kept on with the work, making his influence felt everywhere along the 3 miles (5km) of wall. He was working for God's glory, and spent himself night and day, bubbling over with enthusiasm and determination even when some of his own people, the Tekoite nobles, refused to lift a finger to help. He was aware of enemy spies infiltrating the lines of workmen, dropping words of discontent and despair; but kept his heart constantly uplifted to God. 'The God of heaven will prosper us!' was his infectious refrain.

Sanballat, Tobia and Geshem tried ridicule to break the spirit of the workers: 'With this quality of workmanship, even a fox trying to scramble over the wall would cause it to collapse!' Nothing worked, and they conspired to make a united surprise assault.

Word of the military threat reached Nehemiah. Should he suspend all building operations and prepare for war? His reaction was typical of him as a person and of his way of life.

'We prayed to our God *and posted a guard* day and night.'[1]

To be wide awake, using to the full the intelligence which the Creator had given him and doing it all in a prayerful spirit of dependence on God, was Nehemiah's strength. And it can be ours.

He had half his men doing the work, while the other half hovered over them with spears, shields, bows and armour. 'Don't be afraid of the enemy!' he urged. 'Remember the Lord, who is great and awesome.' Inspired by their prayerful visionary leader, the people worked from the first light of dawn till the stars came out. Prayer reinforced by watching saw them through. Three attempts on Nehemiah's life failed.

Within fifty-two days the wall was complete!

Nehemiah's example is supported by our Lord: '"Watch and pray so that you will not fall into temptation."'[2] The instruction comes through the Apostle Paul: 'Be on your guard; stand firm in the faith; . . . be strong.'[3] Some people pray often but the rest of the time are asleep, off their guard. 'Therefore let us not sleep, as do others; but let us watch and be sober.'[4] Peter adds, 'The end of all things is at hand: be ye therefore sober, and watch unto prayer.'[5] Paul, in Ephesians, urges: 'Praying always with all prayer and supplication in the Spirit, and watching thereunto.'[6]

Against what should we be on the watch?

Firstly, against our own weak points. The angels of Satan scrutinize our words, our reading, the things we feast our eyes on, and even our facial expressions. Satan is searching for weaknesses to exploit, targets on which to launch attacks. We are warned: 'Examine yourselves to see whether you are in the faith; test yourselves.'[7] 'Put to death, therefore, whatever belongs to your earthly nature: sexual immorality, impurity, lust, evil desires and greed . . . rid yourselves of all such things as these: anger, rage, malice, slander and filthy language . . . . Set your minds on things above, not on earthly things. For you died, and your life is now hidden with Christ in God.'[8]

Secondly, we must be on guard against the cares of this life. 'Take heed to yourselves.'[9] 'Be careful, or your hearts will be weighed down with dissipation, drunkenness and the anxieties of life . . . . Be always on the watch.'[10] Prayerfully and watchfully keep your spirit stronger than external circumstances.

Thirdly, watch for the machinations of Satan. 'Be self-controlled and alert. Your enemy the devil prowls around like a roaring lion looking for someone to devour.'[11] Satan has amiable, ingratiating agents everywhere, people who impress as servants of righteousness.[12] Pray for a keen discernment of truth and people. Follow Jesus, and the Bible soundly interpreted.

Which leads to point four: 'Let us fix our eyes on Jesus, the author and perfector of our faith.'[13] ' "Follow me!" ' is His desire for everyone.[14] Watch Him; be alert to weaknesses and dangers within and without; and don't be a follower of people or tradition.

The prayer should often be on our lips: 'Search me, O God, and know my heart; test me and know my anxious thoughts. See if there is any offensive way in me, and lead me in the way everlasting.'[15] Like Nehemiah we should be prayerfully alert and alertly prayerful.

---

[1]Neh. 4:9, emphasis ours. [2]Matt. 26:41. [3]1 Cor. 16:13. [4]1 Thess. 5:6, KJV. [5]1 Peter 4:7, KJV. [6]Eph. 6:18, KJV. [7]2 Cor. 13.5. [8]Col. 3:5, 8, 2, 3. [9]Luke 21:34, KJV. [10]Verses 34, 36. [11]1 Peter 5:8. [12]2 Cor. 11:13-15. [13]Heb. 12:2. [14]John 21:19. [15]Ps. 139:23, 24.

Patterns of prayer

Murray McCheyne wrote: 'What a man is, alone on his knees before God, that he is, and no more.' We never rise higher than our prayers. Since worshipping God is the main business of our lives, and prayer is the most intimate part of that worship, praying both identifies us and reveals our concept of God as nothing else can.

In prayer our daily faithfulness matters. Style and spirit are also of cardinal importance.

• *Some in prayer do not talk to God.* They have developed a quietist, contemplative style. They focus the mind on God's creation, His mercies and blessings, and often achieve a state halfway between sleep and wakefulness. At the end of their musings they feel mystically refreshed. The poet Coleridge recorded that he did not pray 'with moving lips and bended knees', but merely 'composed his spirit to love' and indulged 'a sense of supplication'. But much more is needed.

'This, then, is how you should pray,' says Jesus, and at once turns to actual conversation with God. The Master knows, as no poet or prelate can. God wants us to pour out our thoughts to Him in heartfelt words, instead of retiring into a reverie and calling it prayer. Meditation is superb, when it is part of spoken prayer.

• *Some talk all the time.* They can be impressively eloquent, rapturously carried on the current of their own words. Here Christ's warning applies: ' ''When you pray, do not keep on babbling.'' '[1] Our flow of words does not impress God. In fact, 'when words are many, sin is not absent.'[2] Our very words can generate feelings that neutralize the Spirit's promptings and are mistaken for His guidance. Lots of words inescapably mean 'vain repetitions'.

• *Lifeless praying.* Some prayers are cold; some actually frozen. A duty is being performed, a habit indulged. The praying is feeble and heartless, dry and stale. It will not bring truth, vigour and obedience to the soul.

• *Loudness.* In the chapter entitled 'A vital concept' there was a reference to an American clergyman who was sentenced to two months' imprisonment for 'making too much noise while worshipping'. Many in the act of prayer equate loudness with faith. Noise kindles excitement, which can unleash a storm of feeling, a torrent of words, that make it impossible to discern the Spirit's still, small voice.[3] The thoughtful person will reflect, 'Surely, God is not deaf. He knows what is in my mind before I do. Why should I raise my voice? Is it not perhaps that I'm speaking to myself, working up my emotions? Or addressing people within earshot?' Proper reverence should moderate the tones.

• *Praying in 'tongues'*. J. I. Packer on prayer says, 'Some slip into glossolalia; others make a point of not slipping into it; yet we may all be praying as God means us to do.' In other words, the person who denounces 'tongues' as a gibberish rejected by God and the person who believes 'tongues' to be a spiritual language highly favoured by God are equally guided and approved by God. This paints God in chameleon colours.

Jesus warns us: '"Not everyone who says to me, 'Lord, Lord,' will enter the kingdom of heaven, but only he who does the will of my Father who is in heaven. Many will say to me on that day, 'Lord, Lord, did we not prophesy in your name, and in your name drive out demons and perform many miracles?' Then I will tell them plainly, 'I never knew you. Away from me, you evildoers!'"'[4] This same Jesus also said, '"I am the way and the truth and the life."'[5] When we go to Christ, our supreme Example, we find:

✻ He never 'spoke in tongues'.

✻ When He taught His disciples how to pray, He never so much as hinted at strange sounds having to be heard from them.

'But the day of Pentecost came after His ascension!' some will protest. '*That* is the great historic occasion when the Holy Spirit descended and 120 of Christ's disciples spoke in tongues.'

Yes, the day of Pentecost *is* the historic basis for certain special events. The Bible records: 'When the day of Pentecost came, they were all together in one place. Suddenly a sound like the blowing of a violent wind came from heaven and

filled the whole house where they were sitting. They saw
what seemed to be tongues of fire that separated and came to
rest on each of them. All of them were filled with the Holy
Spirit and began to speak in other tongues as the Spirit enabled them. Now there were staying in Jerusalem God-fearing
Jews from every nation under heaven. When they heard this
sound, a crowd came together in bewilderment, because
each one heard them speaking in his own language. Utterly
amazed, they asked: "Are not all these men who are speaking Galileans? Then how is it that each of us hears them in
his own native language? Parthians, Medes and Elamites;
residents of Mesopotamia, Judea and Cappadocia, Pontus
and Asia, Phrygia and Pamphylia, Egypt and the parts of
Libya near Cyrene; visitors from Rome (both Jews and converts to Judaism); Cretans and Arabs — we hear them declaring the wonders of God in our own tongues!'"[6]

'Tongues' is from the Greek word for tongues and
languages. 'Languages' is the obvious meaning here.

Were the languages spoken known or unknown? 'Each one
heard them speaking in his own language . . . . "How is it
that each of us hears them in his own native language?"'[7]

The Jewish visitors to Jerusalem were astounded. Long
dispersed among other nations, many of them no longer
spoke the Aramaic of Judea. Some came from the east,
Mesopotamia — their native language was that of the Parthians or Medes or Elamites. Others came from the north,
Syria and Asia Minor; yet others from the west and the
south.

This was their experience: 'Utterly amazed, they asked,
"Are not all these men who are speaking Galileans?"'[8] These
were not men of education and culture. Yet they were speaking all these foreign languages with impressive ease and
fluency! '"How is it that each of us hears them in his own
native tongue?"'[9] '"We hear them declaring the wonders of
God in our own tongues!"'[10]

'Amazed and perplexed, they asked one another, "What
does this mean?"'[11] What it meant was that the Holy Spirit
had in an instant given a perfect command of an alien
language, for example, Coptic, to at least one of the disciples,

so that he could now and henceforth 'declare the wonders of God' in that language, witnessing to Christ and His salvation. Each disciple received a specific language gift, which marvellously extended the outreach influence of the disciples and gave momentum to the early Church, enabling it to permeate the then-known world.

The second time we find this language gift for witnessing to people of an alien culture is in Acts 10 and 11. The third time is in Acts 19. There is no reason for assuming that the nature of the gift varied. Acts 2 gives the picture — each speaker used a different language according to the group he was addressing. Latecomers doubtless moved about until they found the group where their own tongue was being spoken. At once they could understand every word. The language barrier was breached; no interpreters were needed.

A conclusion that is inescapable is: for it to be a repetition of the true Pentecost, listeners *must* hear the speech in their own native language.

How different was the church which the Apostle Paul started in Corinth! The congregation had splintered into rival cliques.[12] Instead of being spiritual they were carnal and worldly, given to fighting among themselves.[13] Idolatry and drunkenness were to be found among them — even drunkenness at the Lord's Supper.[14] Members were even suing one another.[15]

And *they*, of all people in the New Testament, often employed language in their meetings that was incomprehensible to the listeners. 'Brothers, stop thinking like children', Paul appealed to them.[16] He said, 'I would rather speak five intelligible words to instruct others than ten thousand words in a tongue.'[17] Sometimes a speaker in this cosmopolitan city would probably say worthwhile things in his native tongue; but the congregation, not understanding the language, was not edified. Firmly regulate and limit this kind of thing, Paul urges. If there is no interpreter, don't allow it at all.[18]

Some Christians live for miracles. They want to feel a supernatural presence and power in their prayers and worship. It thrills them to work up their feelings until they experience tingling, prickling sensations and even bursts of ecstasy. Some need shouting and jumping to achieve this; others find that raising the arms and swaying, hissing or moaning will achieve the desired result. After a while it can happen almost spontaneously. When they break into syllables that are not part of the native language of anyone on earth, they feel that this is a 'heavenly language' or a 'prayer language' especially pleasing to God. One thing is certain: this phenomenon is not identical to the Pentecostal gift of Acts 2!

Some speakers in 'tongues' disapprove of this in public worship. They explain: 'There is so much that is "put on", so much pretended speaking in tongues. And sometimes you know the private life of the person, the lack of spirituality. So I use it for private prayer. It is my own prayer language gift from the Holy Spirit.'

They base this idea on two things: personal experience, and two Scriptures. These are: 'Anyone who speaks in a tongue does not speak to men but to God';[19] and 'If I pray in a tongue, my spirit prays, but my mind is unfruitful'.[20] Both texts are ambiguous. In Acts 2 at Pentecost there was only one possible meaning: '"How is it that each of us hears them in his own native language?"'[21] Gibberish or ecstatic ejaculation cannot be read into this. Some would like 1 Corinthians 14:2 to mean: 'Anyone who speaks in incomprehensible ecstatic sounds addresses not men but God.' But more consistent with Acts 2 is the following meaning: 'Anyone using a language unknown to the congregation is not speaking to them — only God knows what he is saying.' And this agrees with verse 9: 'Unless you speak intelligible words with your tongue, how will anyone know what you are saying? You will just be speaking into the air.'

Verse 14 may be translated: 'If I pray in a tongue (which I understand but you don't), my spirit (mind) prays, but my thoughts bear no fruit in you.' 'If I come to you and speak in tongues, what good will I be to you?'[22]

Remember Paul's problems with their cliques, worldliness, squabbling, immorality and drunkenness. Let us rather concentrate on things that edify others.[23] Gibberish in private prayer will not edify others. Emotion has its place in true prayer, emotionalism does not.

A minister tells how he was pressed by friends to attend a church which was known for the spectacular. There was a great deal of singing and hand-clapping and prayer, punctuated with much emotional ejaculation from the congregation. Emotional tensions grew, culminating in groans, mumblings and incomprehensible words. Some fell to the floor, stiff and glassy-eyed; others had ecstatic jerks. The minister decided to leave.

Later he mused, 'If I had remained in attendance at such meetings and had allowed myself to be persuaded that I "needed an experience in the Spirit", then sooner or later something deep within me would have been stirred. I might have fallen victim to what I verily believe is a delusive physical and psychical experience.' (Harry W. Lowe, *Speaking in Tongues*, Pacific Press Publishing Assoc., USA.)

• *Prayers of command.* We became good friends. I'll call him Ian. We had long conversations about prayer.

'Ian, how did you actually learn the style of prayer that you use?'

'That goes back to my childhood,' he said. 'My pastor invited me to come over every Friday afternoon. I'd go straight from school. I could usually hear his voice from the street. The front door would be locked. I'd go round the back and just walk in. Two or three would be in prayer. I'd shrug off my school books and kneel with them. They'd give no indication that they were aware of my presence. They had open Bibles before them and would quote God's promises to Him and in faith insist that those promises be honoured.'

'What did they pray for?'

'Could be anything. Usually it was for the conversion of souls, or healing from an illness. They prayed by name for everybody they knew — the indifferent, the worldly, people in the grip of vice.'

'How would they pray?'

'They'd weep and plead, remind God that His business was to save souls. They claimed miracles — claimed them by faith. They'd shout the name of someone and say, "God, You love him! I claim the blood of Jesus Christ over him! Break his proud stubborn heart, dear God, and bring him to his knees in repentance!"' '

'And it worked?'

'Sometimes. Fridays they fasted, all day. It was a day devoted to prayer. It was a day of faith. When they prayed for something, they believed they already had it. "God, convert Jones! Thank You, You have converted him! In his heart, though he doesn't know it yet. Even if he blasphemes today, I know You have touched his heart." Let me explain. God can convert souls in their hearts, but they don't know it yet. One day they'll suddenly wake up and know it. Then they'll want to start praying and fighting sin. You don't see it that way, do you?'

'No, I believe the moment a man is converted there is a visible, audible change. Not perfection, but the evidence of a new life will be unmistakable. But tell me, in their prayers were they vocal all the time?'

'No. They'd sometimes fall silent. It made my skin crawl, such a holy silence, interrupted only by a moan or a sibilant intake of breath. Made a great impression on me. Really taught me the art of praying, of faith. Then, after silence, there they were, arms upraised, shouting thanks to God. They had claimed a promise, you see.'

'How did they pray for the sick?'

'The same way. They knew it was God's will to heal everybody. It all depended on faith. So they'd claim His promise to heal, then thank Him for having done so, even though there was no evidence of it. They would speak to the disease and command it to go.'

'In what words?'

'Like, "You filthy demon of deafness, I command you in the name of Jesus to come out of this body! Out, you vile spirit, and never come back in again"' '

'Results?'

'Yes, where there was faith. If the sick person's faith fell short, no. What you must realize is that prayer is conflict, a battle. Paul said to the Colossians, "I want you to know how much I am struggling for you."[24] About Epaphras, who "is always wrestling in prayer for you".[25] A struggle, a wrestling match. See? What does that mean to you?'

'Fervent earnestness, sincerity, and perseverance. The wrestling is a metaphor of whole-heartedness, as opposed to half-heartedness. I feel that if you want to wrestle in prayer, let it be a conflict with yourself, not with God — a battle to accept God's will, which a feeble faith does not want to do.'

'I couldn't agree less! Jacob fought Christ on the banks of the Jabbok. We must fight; God will test us and hang back; He wants us to overcome His . . . what shall I call it, slowness? And we must fight Satan. Christ gave authority to His disciples: '' 'I saw Satan fall like lightning from heaven. I have given you authority . . . to overcome all the power of the enemy.' ''[26] So before I take the pulpit or platform to preach, I pray: ''I bind the forces of darkness! I bind every spirit of doubt. I bind the mouths and minds of those in the audience who would oppose Your message. I bind the devil-forces in Jesus' name. I forbid them in Your name to hinder the passage of Your message into each heart. I also loosen the spirits of the people. I loosen them to receive what You have for them. Give them freedom by the Holy Spirit, an exodus from Satan's bondage!'' See? This gives me confidence, power, the ability to handle opposition. I command in Christ's name. It's great, the effect this has on me, on the entire audience! Remember, to me prayer is warfare!'

• To me, *prayer is surrender*. Most people would agree that it is easier to fight than to surrender our all in faith to the invisible God. If only we could see Him! That privilege was granted to the prophet Isaiah. 'I saw the Lord seated on a throne, high and exalted, and the train of his robe filled the temple. Above him were seraphs, . . . calling to one another: ''Holy, holy, holy is the Lord Almighty; the whole earth is full of his glory.'' At the sound of their voices the doorposts and thresholds shook and the temple was filled with smoke. ''Woe to me!'' I cried. ''I am ruined! For I am a man of unclean lips, and I live among a people of unclean lips, and my eyes have seen the King, the Lord Almighty.'' '[27]

Prayer is the way into God's presence. In that Presence it is right for sinners to feel shattered. Then the glorious truth dawns: 'God *invited* me here! I, a sinner, unreliable, falling infinitely short of the glory of God, am loved by the Almighty!'

How natural then to exclaim: 'Lord, I surrender all! Please bring me into harmony with Thee! No matter what the cost! ''Take my will and make it Thine. It shall be no longer mine. Take my heart, it is Thine own! It shall be Thy royal throne. Take my love, my Lord — I pour at Thy feet its treasure store. Take myself, and I will be ever, only, all for Thee!''' (Frances Ridley Havergal.)

This is the supreme miracle of God's grace.

Selwyn Hughes, founder of the 'Crusade for World Revival', says: 'I see prayer as self surrender. It is a commitment to develop a *relationship* with God rather than just asking Him for things.'

> Not I, but Christ, be honoured, loved, exalted;
> Not I, but Christ, be seen, be known, be heard;
> Not I, but Christ, in every look and action,
> Not I, but Christ, in every thought and word.
>
> Christ, only Christ! no idle words e'er falling,
> Christ, only Christ; no needless, bustling sound;
> Christ, only Christ; no self-important bearing;
> Christ, only Christ; no trace of 'I' be found.
> — *Fannie E. Bolton*

---

[1]Matt. 6:7. [2]Prov. 10:19. [3]1 Kings 19:12. [4]Matt. 7:21-23. [5]John 14:6. [6]Acts 2:1-11. [7]Verses 6, 8. [8]Verse 7. [9]Verse 8. [10]Verse 11. [11]Verse 12. [12]1 Cor. 1:10-17. [13]1 Cor. chapter 6. [14]1 Cor. chapters 5, 6, 11. [15]Chapter 6. [16]1 Cor. 14:20. [17]Verse 19. [18]Verse 28. [19]1 Cor. 14:2. [20]Verse 14. [21]Acts 2:8, 11. [22]1 Cor. 14:6. [23]Verse 19. [24]Col. 2:1. [25]Col. 4:12. [26]Luke 10:18, 19. [27]Isa. 6:1-5.

Can Satan answer 'Christian' prayer?

Medieval tradition and superstition gave us a picture of Satan as a hideous monster with hoofs, horns, pitchfork, barbed tail and breath of flames. Far from minding, he loves to be depicted grotesquely — caricatures are mocked by intelligent people. Disbelief and confusion result.

Actually, he was once a glorious angelic being in God's presence. Under the figure of the king of Tyre, a description of him is given by the prophet Ezekiel. Satan was wise and beautiful;[1] he was in the garden of God, resplendent, pure and holy.[2] He rebelled against his Maker,[3] and there was war in heaven, ending in his expulsion and that of his angel followers.[4]

He is still at war, battling to frustrate the Gospel. 'Satan himself masquerades as an angel of light'[5] to turn people away from God and His truths. He deceives people of charm and influence and uses them as agents. 'It is not surprising, then, if his servants masquerade as servants of righteousness.'[6] ' ''False Christs and false prophets will appear and perform great signs and miracles to deceive even the elect — if that were possible.'' '[7] 'I saw three evil spirits . . . . They are spirits of demons performing miraculous signs.'[8] 'Your enemy the devil prowls around like a roaring lion looking for someone to devour.'[9]

He is powerfully at work in every pagan religion and in Christianity. So massive and pervasive is his influence that the Bible calls him the god of this world.[10] A god is an object of faith and worship. Satan is worshipped, directly and indirectly, so that all but a 'remnant' obey his inventions.[11]

This 'angel of light' and his fellow angels cannot be expected to ignore any of God's methods of uplifting and saving souls — including prayer. In true prayer to the devil's divine Enemy, the leader of the apostate hosts is defeated. So he tries to misdirect believers, leading them to pray in false ways.

In his inimitable style, C. S. Lewis in *Screwtape Letters** illuminates one way of doing this. He has a fallen angel say, 'Whenever they are attending to the Enemy Himself we are defeated, but there are ways of preventing them from doing so. The simplest is to turn their gaze away from Him towards themselves. Keep them watching their own minds and trying to produce *feelings* there by the action of their own wills. When they meant to ask Him for charity, let them, instead, start trying to manufacture charitable feelings for themselves and not notice that this is what they are doing. When they meant to pray for courage, let them really be trying to feel brave. When they say they are praying for forgiveness, let them be trying to feel forgiven. *Teach them to estimate the value of each prayer by their success in producing the desired feeling;* and let them never suspect how much success or failure of that kind depends on whether they are well or ill, fresh or tired, at the moment . . . . Don't forget to use the 'heads I win, tails you lose' argument. If the thing he prays for doesn't happen, then that is one more proof that petitionary prayers don't work; if it does happen he will, of course, be able to see some physical causes which led up to it, and "therefore it would have happened anyway", and thus *a granted prayer becomes just as good a proof as a denied one that prayers are ineffective.*' (*The Screwtape Letters* — emphasis ours.)

True prayer, humbly reverent, sincere, earnest and biblical, breathing as it does the spirit of Jesus Christ, enrages and frustrates Satan. He is unable to break in. Almighty power shields the supplicant. ' "The eternal God is your refuge, and underneath are the everlasting arms. He will drive out your enemy before you." '[12] It is an awe-inspiring experience, sacred and life-giving. 'He who dwells in the shelter of the Most High will rest in the shadow of the Almighty . . . . His faithfulness will be your shield and rampart.'[13]

Satan can neither interfere with nor answer such prayers.

But what if the prayer is faithless, insincere? What if it is

---

* *Lewis wrote to unveil the strategy of Satan. Hence, when the demon speaks of 'the Enemy Himself' — he means God!*

unbiblical, or centred in self? What if, despite Christian terminology, it is 'pagan'?[14]

Then Satan is not enraged, does not tremble, is not kept at bay.

Posing as an 'angel of light', a messenger from the Almighty, he could overshadow that supplicant with his presence and power. The one praying could experience powerful emotions, deep movings of the spirit — but whose spirit? Judas Iscariot was in Christ's presence night and day for about two years — but the wrong spirit moved in him and worked his ruin.

What about the powerful, spirit-filled Christians who have been zealous workers for Christ and eventually protest: ' ' ' 'Lord, Lord, did we not prophesy in your name, and in your name drive out demons and perform many miracles?' Then I will tell them plainly, 'I never knew you. (So Christ was not the one who responded to their prayers!) Away from me, you evildoers!' ' ' '[15] Something was wrong there! In spite of their multitudinous prayers and dynamic Gospel ministry, they are denied heaven. The prayer life which had seemed to them and others so blessed in spirit and even with miracles in Christ's name, had been anointed by a spirit alien to Christ's.

Imagine a person like the one we have just read about in the book of Matthew. The devil takes possession of her body, making her sick. She cries to God for help and Satan bends over her and impresses her with the need to go to certain 'healing meetings'. She goes and when those desiring healing are called forward, she approaches the 'healer'. While he prays for and touches her, Satan suddenly ceases to exercise his evil power — she is 'healed'! It is loudly proclaimed that a miracle has been wrought. The healed woman is overwhelmed with a sense of God's blessing and power through the healer, and throws in her influence with him. His ministry is strengthened by her testimony of miraculous power. Tragically, he is also a person similar to that described in Matthew 7:21-23, as deluded and misdirected as she. In the invisible war, Satan is the gainer. He uses even miracles to build up his agents to greater usefulness for his kingdom.

How vital then, beyond words to convey, that we not be Christians of the above variety! Can we obtain certainty that we are not? Not subjectively, by simply declaring that we are not, but *demonstrably*?

God's Word can help us. Let us examine Matthew 7:21-23.

• These Christians are passionate for God: 'Lord, Lord!'

• They work for God, prophesying, performing many miracles, doing command praying and exorcizing devils. Their ministry is in word and power! And their indisputable driving out of demons seems to authenticate that they are servants of the Creator-God!

• They fail to do 'the will of my Father who is in heaven'. They ignore certain of God's requirements. The words are there and the power is there; but their obedience is selective. They may be charming, talented and exuding love — but God pronounces them disobedient.

'Why did you not obey the Lord?' Samuel demanded of King Saul.

'But I *did* obey the Lord!' Saul protested, and echoes of this 'sincerity' are found in Matthew 7:21-23.

The prophet replied: '"Does the Lord delight in burnt offerings and sacrifices as much as in obedience to the voice of the Lord? To obey is better than sacrifice, and to heed is better than the fat of rams."' [16]

'Whoever keeps the whole law, and yet stumbles at just one point, is guilty of breaking all of it. For he who said, "Do not commit adultery," also said, "Do not murder." If you do not commit adultery but do commit murder, you have become a law-breaker. Speak and act as those who are going to be judged by the law that gives freedom.' [17]

We are not saved by keeping the Ten Commandments, God's great moral law. We are saved by grace; yet our state of grace will be evidenced by obedience.

---

[1]Ezek. 28:12. [2]Verses 13-15. [3]Isa. 14:12. [4]Rev. 12:7-12. [5]2 Cor. 11:14. [6]Verse 15. [7]Matt. 24:24. [8]Rev. 16:13, 14. [9]1 Peter 5:8. [10]2 Cor. 4:4, KJV. [11]Rev. 12:17, KJV. [12]Deut. 33:27. [13]Ps. 91:1, 4. [14]Matt. 6:7. [15]Matt. 7:22, 23. [16]1 Sam. 15:19-22. [17]James 2:10-12.

Why some prayers seem ignored

There can be no doubt about the Lord's ability to answer prayer. '"Ah, Sovereign Lord, you have made the heavens and the earth by your great power and outstretched arm. Nothing is too hard for you."'[1] We see the power of God in every blade of grass, in the tiniest insect, as well as in the sun and other colossal stars.

Is God willing to grant our prayer requests? The basic truth about prayer is that God is even more ready to listen to our prayers than we are to utter them. And He is more eager to give than we are to ask. 'He who did not spare his own Son, but gave him up for us all — how will he not also, along with him, graciously give us all things?'[2] 'God so loved the world' that He gave — in effect, emptied heaven of its joy and glory — to help humanity back to life. '"I am not saying that I will ask the Father on your behalf. No, the Father himself loves you."'[3] There is a divine eagerness in love. God's desire is to answer prayer.

Why then is it a matter of common observation that many prayers are not answered? At least not according to the terms of the request?

• 'When you ask, you do not receive, because you ask with *wrong motives*, that you may spend what you get on your pleasures.'[4] The wrong motives can be varied; but usually selfishness is involved, or pride. To answer such a prayer would be to honour the motive behind it; and for the sake of our character refinement God cannot do that. Our hearts should be frankly and honestly scrutinized, using the spotlight of the character of the Lord Jesus Christ.

• Nothing hinders prayer as effectively as sin. 'Surely the arm of the Lord is not too short to save, nor his ear too dull to hear. But your iniquities have separated you from your God; your sins have hidden his face from you, so that he will not hear.'[5]

Sins can be blatant deeds of transgression — 'I know this

is wrong, but I want to do it.' Or they can be negligence in learning the will of God. The mind is simply closed to un-welcome truths, inconvenient commands. This evasiveness is not admitted to oneself — a blind spot has developed, and one has learned to be comfortable with it. Some say, 'I have a simple faith; that's all I need.' A thought they don't want to acknowledge even to themselves is: 'I'm not going to compli-cate my life with difficult things. I don't want to hear this. If the judgement should put me in a bad light, I want to be able to plead honest ignorance. Surely God would not condemn me if I were honestly ignorant, sincerely unconvinced!' Dis-daining sophistry, we must be honest with our Maker. He wants us to be avid for His truth. Neglecting opportunities to know God's mind and conform to His requirements is a basic sin.

'If I had cherished sin in my heart, the Lord would not have listened.'[6] When the disciples were confronted by a man with a mentally handicapped son they found themselves bereft of all power. 'Lord, we prayed. Nothing happened! Why?' They had been indulging a spirit of pettiness and self-glorification, which tainted their prayers. Because of their spirit they were in God's sight unbelieving and perverse.[7]

• Indulging an *unforgiving spirit* is another perversity. '"When you stand praying, if you hold anything against anyone, forgive him, so that your Father in heaven may for-give you your sins."'[8] One should not wait for the other per-son to make overtures of peace. Even if he is hard and harsh, you can pray for him, ask the Lord to forgive him, forgive him yourself; and at the same time be humbly ready for any errand God may have for you. Jesus prayed for the Roman soldiers who crucified Him: '"Father, forgive them, for they do not know what they are doing."'[9]

A forgiving spirit does not require losing touch with reality and truth. Many varieties of behaviour go by the name of forgiveness, and not all of them are admirable. One kind says, 'As a Christian I forgive her, but I shall never speak to her again.' Another says, 'I forgive you, Jones, and I will pray for you'; which is guaranteed to inflame Jones's darkest and most evil passions. Or: 'I'll forgive you on condition you say you are sorry and never do it again.' Man dare not demand repentance as a condition for *bestowing* pardon; yet repentance remains an essential condition for *receiving* it.

We have our own repenting to do, and our heavenly Father will forgive. No one living is wholly innocent. Our God does not 'clear the guilty', yet He is ' "The Lord, the Lord, the compassionate and gracious God, slow to anger, abounding in love and faithfulness" '[10] in whom a spirit of forgiveness is immortalized.

* ' "These men had set up *idols in their hearts* . . . . Should I let them enquire of me at all?" '[11] A thing, or another person, can be given precedence to God . . . with disastrous results. Giving first place to a parent, a child, a wife or a husband makes one unworthy of Christ.[12] One can even put one's Church before God!

The supplicant in sincerity will put God first, incomparably so. He or she will ask God's help in this. 'Search me, O God, and know my heart; test me and know my anxious thoughts. See if there is any offensive way in me, and lead me in the way everlasting.'[13]

* 'Husbands, in the same way be considerate as you live with your wives, and treat them with respect as the weaker partner and as heirs with you of the gracious gift of life, so that nothing will hinder your prayers.'[14] *Ungracious behaviour* towards the one closest to us will hinder our prayers.

Doing no violence to 1 Corinthians 13, we can positively say: 'Jesus is patient, kind, never indulging envy, never boasting or proud. He is never rude or self-seeking, not easily angered, nurturing not a single grudge. Nothing that is even vaguely tainted appeals to Him; His life is built on truth. He always protects, always trusts, hopes, perseveres. When needed, Jesus never proves to be a broken reed — He is staunch, utterly reliable.'

The home is a good proving-ground for the genuineness of Christian character that gives wings to our prayers.

* The adage, 'A person wrapped up in himself or herself makes a very small package,' can apply to prayer.

This lesson is intrinsic to Christ's parable: ' "Suppose one of you has a friend, and he goes to him at midnight and says,

'Friend, lend me three loaves of bread, because a friend of mine on a journey has come to me, and I have nothing to set before him.' Then the one inside answers, 'Don't bother me. The door is already locked, and my children are with me in bed. I can't get up and give you anything.' I tell you, though he will not get up and give him the bread because he is his friend, yet because of the man's persistence he will get up and give him as much as he needs.'"[15]

What lent bold persistency to the pleas was this: he asked so that he could give. He wasn't saying, 'I'm hungry, so do leave your cosy bed, light a candle and rummage around for something to still my pangs.' No — 'Please *lend* me bread; I'll repay you. I want it for someone in need.' The man inside is shamed, and reflects: '*He* left his warm bed to help another. *He* embarrassed himself by rousing me from my sleep. He's not asking to get, but to share. And here I'm being churlish, crude, rude. I *must* get up and give him all he needs!'

The lesson is by contrast. The man inside represents God; but God is *not* reluctant, self-indulgent, rude. How much *more* then will God give when you are asking so that you may share! And unselfish prayer lends boldness and persistency to the supplications.

If prayers are steeped in self, they are not offered 'in the name of Jesus' — His spirit, His concern and motives. It is well to ask oneself: 'Am I asking so that I might bring honour to God? Am I an agent of God's mercy and wisdom towards another soul?' When we harmonize with God, Jesus says: '"So I say to you: Ask and it will be given to you."'[16]

In substance, one can say: • Our asking must be according to God's will.[17] • We must ask for the things God has specifically promised. • Whatever we receive must be used in doing His will. The conditions met, the answer is certain. '"Whatever you ask for in prayer, believe that you have received it, and it will be yours."'[18]

---

[1]Jer. 32:17. [2]Rom. 8:32. [3]John 16:26, 27. [4]James 4:3, emphasis ours. [5]Isa. 59:1, 2. [6]Ps. 66:18. [7]Matt. 17:14-21. [8]Mark 11:25. [9]Luke 23:34. [10]Exod. 34:6. [11]Ezek. 14:3, emphasis ours. [12]Matt. 10:37. [13]Ps. 139:23, 24. [14]1 Peter 3:7. [15]Luke 11:5-8. [16]Verse 9. [17]1 John 5:14. [18]Mark 11:24.

Prayer-power techniques?

Jesus faced many problems. It is unlikely that His parents ever really understood Him. On one occasion they deserted Him, apparently in the belief that He was with another family. He was unpopular with His nation's leaders, who declared Him public enemy number one. His disciples were unreliable, one betraying Him, another disowning Him, and all of them leaving Him in the lurch. Influential people spread the foolish and groundless slander that He was a glutton and a drunkard. Spies dogged His footsteps, as did poverty — He Himself said He had no place to rest His head. He was *the* Man of Sorrows.

Why didn't He solve these problems? Didn't He know about what American TV evangelists call 'prayer-power'? Didn't He know that 'prayer is the greatest power in the universe, available to you for solving your personal problems'? Didn't He know that by 'shooting love thoughts' at His enemies He could dramatically change their attitude towards Him? That a believer's life should be one of joy and victory, not sorrows, depressing problems and tears?

According to the premises of the prayer-power movement within Christianity, Jesus obviously did not set a good example in prosperity and the solving of His own problems.

Prayer-power is a philosophy based on Jesus' words: ' "The Kingdom of God is within you." '[1] This is taken to mean that the Creator has laid up within your mind and personality powers and abilities which you can tap to solve your problems. It is the greatest power available to the individual. It works by faith, for Christ said you will get anything you set your faith on. It works through the subconscious. It has to do with vibrations that you send out in prayer, which connect you with specific people and with God. Employing a force inherent in a spiritual universe, it changes people's attitudes and amazingly stimulates creative ideas. The technique for getting these results is affirmation, positive thoughts — never allow a negative thought into your mind. Visualize the results you want and hold that 'picture' in your mind until it 'actualizes'.

A businessman has a business and a personal crisis. He says, 'No power on earth can save me'; but learns how to apply prayer-power techniques and ultimately everything works out so well that he says, 'Every problem can be solved and solved right if you pray.'

A married couple, members of a prayer-power church, are out jogging. They pass a magnificent mansion, an extravagant monument to worldly success. The man turns to his wife and exclaims, 'What I wouldn't give to own that!'

'That's no problem,' she replies, her voice resounding with sincerity and confidence. 'Jesus said you can have anything. Put your faith to work. In Jesus' name claim that house as your property!'

A woman discovers that her husband is drifting away from her into another woman's arms. She is told how to imprint a picture on her mind of restored harmony with her husband and make it part of her prayers. At this juncture her husband tells her he wants a divorce. 'I'll co-operate,' she says, 'provided we postpone the decision for ninety days.'

Night after night he is missing but she visualizes him in his favourite chair, reading. By faith she sees him pottering about, doing the dishes, and the two of them playing golf. She holds on to this picture and then one night . . . there he is in person! Things develop to the point where he reads to her, then he proposes a game of golf.

'This is the ninetieth day,' she eventually announces.

He is puzzled. 'What do you mean, the ninetieth day?'

She explains.

'Don't be silly,' he responds. 'Why would I ever dream of leaving you?'

So the formula has proved 'a powerful mechanism'. This is, it is explained, 'creative prayer'. Prayer power is a 'manifestation of energy'. It will even retard the ageing process. 'Prayer driven deeply into your subconscious can remake you. It releases and keeps power flowing freely.'

Prayer, we are told, should be studied from 'an efficiency

point of view'; we should be striving for greater results by varying the prayer pattern or formula. Remind yourself that you are dealing with 'the most tremendous power in the world when you pray'. Experiment, practise new skills — 'any method through which you can stimulate the power of God to flow into your mind is legitimate and usable.'

These are striking claims. One man started a church of about ten people on these principles, and within three years had 4,000 adherents. Many priests and ministers have derided this as a 'prosperity cult'. Is this movement one that 'correctly handles the word of truth'?[2]

Let us take a close look at Luke 17:21: '"The kingdom of God is within you."' Jesus utters these words while addressing the Pharisees, His sworn enemies. They wanted to know when the kingdom of God would come, by which they meant the overthrow of the Roman armies and the liberation of Israel. They wanted a 'prayer-power' kind of solution — problems solved, prosperity aplenty!

Jesus indicated that their 'picturization' (visualization) of things was mistaken. They would discover the kingdom of God, if at all, in their own hearts — the kingdom of grace. This was a spiritual kingdom: victory over self and sin, surrender to God, conversion. As He told the eminent Pharisee Nicodemus, '"I tell you the truth, unless a man is born again, he cannot see the kingdom of God."'[3] Those in the kingdom become like the Father in character. Righteousness is the essence of God's kingdom of grace.

This kingdom has nothing to do with a power in the subconscious that can be projected in vibrations to solve all our temporal problems.

The female jogger said to her husband, 'Jesus said you can have anything. Put your faith to work. In Jesus' name claim that house as your property!' This is a reference to Mark 11:24: '"Therefore I tell you, whatever you ask for in prayer, believe that you have received it, and it will be yours."' Reread the details about this text in the chapter 'Blank cheque texts examined'. It does not support the prayer-power concept. If Christ's disciples had correctly understood these words and held on to them, they would not have lost their faith three days later.

When you, by faith, 'claim' someone's house as your own and you prayerfully 'visualize' that outcome until it 'actualizes', what happens to the principle of 'Not my will, but Thy will be done' which was the keynote of Christ's life? The thoughtful reader will say, 'The two concepts can never be reconciled. You're trying by mental processes to influence events as you want them. Christ's way was not to try to influence the Father's thoughts but to discover the Father's decisions and co-operate with them.'

Real prayer does not adopt any strategy that in the final analysis implies, 'My will must emerge from this.' When the prayer-power school was castigated for discarding the 'God's will be done' approach, they simply tacked those words on to their procedures — procedures which must always be in conflict with the surrender approach.

True prayer is surrender to God's mind.

If I were Satan I should do my utmost to promote the prayer-power scheme, seeing clearly how it is at odds with the spirit of Christ, the Man of Sorrows. To promote this reliance on techniques for getting what you want, I'd use my network of angels endowed with superhuman intelligence and vast experience in dealing with the human mind. We'd soon develop lots of case studies and remarkable evidence. We'd win over the very elect of God with miracles![4] This movement would be popular in the extreme — a power residing in humans, vibrations setting cosmic forces in motion. My angel spirit guides could excite people marvellously and keep them from searching out and obeying the Creator's truth.

True prayer is an inestimable blessing. The power is not in vibrations or the subconscious mind. The power is not even in our prayers — it is in the God to whom we direct our prayers. Prayer is not a setting in motion of inherent spiritual forces — it is the opening of our heart to God. We open our hearts to help us receive our heavenly Father. Prayer does not bring God down to our picturization and techniques; it lifts us up to God's plans for us, based on infinite love and wisdom. This opening of the heart to God requires acknowledging our total lack of power, our abysmal need. It requires humility and surrender. We 'lose our life' into our Father's hands. That is the way of blessing.

Faith in God's omnipotence and goodness is needed. Prayer is the 'key' in the hand of faith. Faith turns to God in prayer; in prayer my heart opens to God in confession, trust and thanksgiving. The Holy Spirit can take over more completely in me. He has access to all heaven's resources. As I unceasingly pray and diligently watch, God's perfect plans can become reality in my character and life. Satan will use all his angelic power to confuse and misdirect. He will powerfully strive to obstruct the way to the mercy-seat of God. As we hold on in faith, the Holy Spirit will use whatever wisdom and power may be necessary to protect and help us. Nothing that in any way concerns our peace is too small for our Father to take seriously, because He loves us.

A minister tells of a woman who had been a Christian but had given it all up. He asked her why she had withdrawn from Christ. She said she no longer believed the Bible.

'I've put its promises to the test and found them untrue,' she said.

'Which promises?'

'The promises about prayer.'

'And those are?'

'Doesn't it say in the Bible, ''Whatever you ask for in faith, you'll receive''?'

'Yes, something like that.'

'Well, I asked and fully expected to get what I asked for. But I didn't get it. See? The promise failed.'

He pondered a moment. 'Was the promise made to you?'

'Of course. The Bible is for all Christians, isn't it?'

'No, God carefully defines who the people are whose prayers, prayed in the Holy Spirit, He will answer. Let's read 1 John 3:21, 22: ''Dear friends, if our hearts do not condemn us, we have confidence before God and receive from him anything we ask, because we obey his commands and do what pleases him.'' Now, dear sister, *were you keeping God's commandments and doing what pleases Him?'* Crestfallen, she found it impossible to say she had been.

God is utterly unimpressed with prayer-power techniques. He looks for humility, trust, obedience, self-forgetfulness and a consuming love of truth. '"I live in a high and holy place, but also with him who is contrite and lowly in spirit."'[5]

---

[1]Luke 17:21. [2]2 Tim. 2:15. [3]John 3:3. [4]Matt. 24:24. [5]Isa. 57:15.

The Lord's Prayer

'The Sovereign Lord has given me an instructed tongue, to know the word that sustains the weary. He wakens me morning by morning, wakens my ear to listen like one being taught.'[1]

The Lord Jesus Christ received a fresh baptism of the Holy Spirit every day. This happened in the early morning when He was alone with His Father in prayer. These occasions were often out in nature — He loved praying on a hill or on a mountain. As He prayed His soul and His lips were anointed with grace by the Holy Spirit; so that all through the day as He spoke to people about heavenly things He would say exactly the right things. '"For the one whom God has sent speaks the words of God, to him God gives the Spirit without limit."'[2]

No wonder Christ's disciples were so deeply impressed by His prayers! They had never seen or heard of anyone whose communion with God was so complete and sustained. Never did He seem to have the Father out of His mind. One day they came upon Him while He was praying. Seeming unaware of their presence, He continued while they listened in awe. When He rose to His feet they exclaimed, 'Lord, teach us to pray!'

He was more than willing. First He repeated the thoughts that would become known as the 'Lord's Prayer', earlier made known in the Sermon on the Mount.

On that occasion He first stressed motive. Why pray? Some loved to pray in such a way as '"to be seen by men"'.[3] False motives could be superstition, to curry favour with God; or pride, to be a notch higher than other people; or to get hold of divine power for pursuing personal goals; or to change God's mind; or force of habit. The only true motive is to draw so close to the heavenly Father that we harmonize with Him.

Secondly, prayer should not be a torrent of words and repetition. '"When you pray, do not keep on babbling like pagans, for they think they will be heard because of their many words." [4] We tend to be impressed with eloquent prayer; God is not. He reads the heart. Our prayers should be vocalized, thoughtful sincerity.

Some in prayer give the Lord up-to-the-minute information or news. 'Lord, Smith has lost his job and he and his family are having a hard time. He has applied for another job, but there will be other applications too. He's feeling low in spirit. Please give him . . . .' Didn't the Lord know all this — before Smith knew it himself? Aren't we praying thoughtlessly when we give God information? Isn't it better to say, 'Father, as You know, Smith has . . . .' '"Your Father knows what you need before you ask him."' [5]

- Christ starts His model prayer with the word *'Father'*. [6] Human fathers are fallible and do err. The true Father is all love and wisdom. So tender are His feelings towards us that He invites us to call him 'Father'. And He calls us His children. He is holy and exalted; we, of the dust. Yet He honours us with a precious relationship with Himself. We may exclaim, 'I am not an orphan! I have a Father whose love rests on me every moment of every day.'

- '"'Our Father *in heaven*.'"' [7] His address is 'The Universe'. He is the Supreme One who created everything 'in heaven and on earth, visible and invisible'. [8] He is before everything and responsible for everything but sin. Without Him there is no life. What a marvel that He should be so humble that He calls us His children and gave His life for us!

- '"'Hallowed be your name.'"' [9] This is a prayer that the Lord's holiness might be seen in us — our deportment, words, deeds and spirit. We want to honour Him, and pray for divine help to achieve this. These words also mean: 'May many surrender their lives into Your Hands, Father. May they represent You in character and truth. May Your name be honoured by our lives.'

- '"'Your kingdom come.'"' [10] This acknowledges that the world desperately needs the second coming, or advent, of Jesus. We yearn for that day, live for it, and call it our 'blessed hope'. [11] 'Come, Lord Jesus,' we say, 'and do not delay!' [12]

• ''''May your will be done on earth as it is in heaven.''''[13] Multiplied millions have 'exchanged the truth of God for a lie, and worshipped and served created things rather than the Creator.'[14] Earth is a planet in rebellion. God's Ten Commandments, presented to man in God's own handwriting, are trodden underfoot even in popular Christianity. 'It is time for you to act, O Lord; your law is being broken.'[15] 'May the time soon come when Your will alone will be done on this planet!'

This is the first half of the model prayer. The one who prays concentrates here on the Fatherhood of God, His ownership of the universe, His character, His kingdom, His will and His glory. We bring God our adoration and identify with Him in His purposes.

• Now we begin to think of ourselves, our spiritual and temporal needs. ''''Give us each day our daily bread.''''[16] Lord, as the Israelites daily needed manna for forty years to keep alive, so I need Your care. Please keep this mortal body going, and help me to live in harmony with its laws — Your laws of life and health. Watch over me, Father. At the same time I realize that I can't live on material food alone — I need every word You have spoken, every morsel of spiritual nourishment. Help me to receive it in Your Scriptures and in a life of fellowship with You — in faith and in obedience, in prayer and in witnessing for you; in thanksgiving and in love for You.

• ''''Forgive us our sins, for we also forgive everyone who sins against us.''''[17] By Your grace, Lord, I hold no grudge but forgive all who hurt or harm me. Please help me to do this honestly. Thank You for enabling grace. And please forgive my sins of commission and omission. Show me what I need to confess . . . .

• ''''Lead us not into temptation.''''[18] Thank You for leading me. How I need that guidance! Lead me in obedience, and in every decision of life. You know the sins that so easily beset and entangle me.[19] You know how easily bad desires drag me away and entice me.[20] Please lead me clear of my weak points, my temptations! Save me from myself!

Deliver me from the evil within, and from the evil angel who is trying to lead me astray . . . .

After the model prayer, Jesus told the story dealt with in the chapter 'Why some prayers seem ignored'. The first lesson is that our prayers are not to be merely a selfish asking; we are to think of others and of the glory of God.

The second lesson is the need to persevere in prayer. Prayer's main purpose is to bring us into harmony with God, and this may take time. Changes may be needed in us. There may be sin, or neglect of duty towards God. We may have been talking in a hopeless, discouraged way, instead of dwelling on the goodness and compassion of God. We may have been doing things that weaken us — bad habits, questionable practices, self-pity, complaining — things that only make us weak and bring no strength to those around us.

Having told the parable with its pointed lessons, Jesus speaks of a Gift from heaven. '"If you . . . know how to give good gifts to your children, how much more will your Father in heaven give the Holy Spirit to those who ask him!"'[21]

We might ask for lesser gifts, but never can we ask for a greater gift than the Holy Spirit. The Holy Spirit brings all other blessings in His train. The Holy Spirit received is the impartation of the life of Christ. He can bestow on us 'a crown of beauty instead of ashes, the oil of gladness instead of mourning, and a garment of praise instead of a spirit of despair'.[22]

We said earlier that when Jesus prayed His soul and lips were anointed with grace by the Holy Spirit. How much more do we need that! It is not enough to model our prayers on the Lord's Prayer. Like our Lord, we need to pray by the inspiration of the Holy Spirit. 'Pray in the Spirit.'[23]

'The Spirit helps us in our weakness. We do not know what we ought to pray, but the Spirit himself intercedes for us with groans that words cannot express. And he who searches our hearts knows the mind of the Spirit, because the Spirit intercedes for the saints in accordance with God's will.'[24] The thoughts here brought to view are:

- We suffer from 'weakness'. If we take to heart the

teachings of Jesus on prayer, we have taken a giant step forward. But there will still be times when 'we do not know what we ought to pray for' — this is our 'weakness' or deficiency. We are limited in knowledge, wisdom and experience. The Holy Spirit knows, where we are confounded.

• The Holy Spirit can inspire us to pray beyond our normal thinking.

• Words may fail us as we try to express the faith, love and submission prompted by the Holy Spirit. We may even stammer, grope or groan.

• The Father searches our hearts, and finds there perfect harmony with the divine will; because our minds have blended with the mind of the Holy Spirit.

Praying in the Spirit means praying as Jesus would, were He in your place. He was controlled by the motive of honouring His heavenly Father, not just while in prayer but in all His life. He loved His Father. His faith in the Father was perfect; hence His confidence in the Father's will for Him was perfect. Unselfishness and concern for others characterized Jesus' prayers.

This spirit does not spring from man's nature. Only the Holy Spirit can instil in us the spirit of Christ. That should be the central thrust in every prayer. Our desire is to pray not in our spirit, but in the Spirit . . . as the Master would, in our circumstances.

---

[1]Isa. 50:4. [2]John 3:34. [3]Matt. 6:5. [4]Verse 7. [5]Verse 8. [6]Luke 11:2. [7]Matt. 6:9; Luke 11:2, NIV footnote. [8]Col. 1:16. [9]Luke 11:2. [10]Verse 2. [11]Titus 2:13. [12]Rev. 22:20. [13]Matt. 6:10; Luke 11:2, NIV footnote. [14]Rom. 1:25. [15]Ps. 119:126. [16]Luke 11:3. [17]Verse 4. [18]Verse 4. [19]Heb. 12:1. [20]James 1:14. [21]Luke 11:13. [22]Isa. 61:3. [23]Eph. 6:18. [24]Rom. 8:26, 27.

Guidance through prayer

'Your ears will hear a voice behind you, saying, ''This is the way; walk in it.'' '[1]

Believers have been sighing for that voice ever since the marvellous promise was made. Imagine a young person agonizing over a career crisis, or a life companion. Must major surgery be undergone or refused? Accept this offer on my house? Move to a new address? Let this friendship go? Enter into litigation? Is it God's will for me to do this . . . or that? How can I know?

John Stott says that, after prayer, 'I have found it vital to check three things when faced with a decision. First, is there anything in the Bible against what I am considering doing? Second, what are the circumstances? Third, have I peace in my heart about it? If all three are there, I find I am on course.'

This is a laudable step forward compared to the usual procedure: 'I like doing this and I've got a chance to do it, so why not?' Let's examine the three points.

First, is there any contra-indication in the Bible? A very sound consideration indeed! Our Lord Jesus sets the standard by saying, '''''Man does not live on bread alone, but on every word that comes from the mouth of God.'''''[2] We should measure every tentative decision against the Bible. But then two questions are unavoidable.

• Is our knowledge of the Bible such that we can say, 'I have hidden your word in my heart that I might not sin against you.'[3] Have we been striving assiduously to get the Word of God into our minds? A sound and extensive knowledge of the Bible can help, sometimes remarkably, to influence our decision. Perhaps we need to make a commitment to the Lord: 'I will not neglect your word.'[4]

• Is my interpretation of God's Word slanted by habit, social convention, or religious but unbiblical tradition? This is the problem of having developed blind spots. For example, the Bible teaches that our body must be treated with a sense of spiritual responsibility. 'Do you not know that your body is a temple of the Holy Spirit . . . ? You are not your own.'[5] 'So whether you eat or drink or whatever you do, do it all for the glory of God.'[6] Would you light a cigarette and sit puffing in church? Should a believer smoke at all, in view of the fact that his body is a shrine for the Holy Spirit? I say once in fifty years would be once too often, but many adherents of Christianity do so quite blithely. One man even told me, 'I know the Bible says I must eat or drink or whatever to the glory of God. So I smoke to the glory of God!' To my question whether he would lie or steal to the glory of God he declined an answer, as he did to the question of whether he would smoke a cigarette while engaged in prayer.

Interpreting the Bible according to the mind of the Holy Spirit is a life-or-death matter. Enslaving habits, social conventions and Church traditions that depart from Bible teaching should be allowed no influence. We should pray daily for a true understanding of God's Word.

Now, the second test to apply — 'what are the circumstances?' Circumstances should never be allowed to override Bible standards. That would be a case of situation ethics — adapting your principles to what is happening around you. Yet wisdom should be applied to the complexities of situations. Responsibility, common sense and Christian love must be given due weight.

Third test: 'Do I have peace in my heart about it?' The human conscience is very complacent and accommodating, unless trained and strictly disciplined by the Scriptures. 'Peace in my heart' can be very subjective and perilous. 'There is a way that seems right to a man, but in the end it leads to death.'[7]

Another religious leader advises: Once we sense God's will in a matter, we should apply three tests. First, do we have a deep inner sense of God's will? Second, is there a witness from the Word, a relevant text that comes as a token? Third, is there an independent witness through an incident or a person uninfluenced by us? When all three agree, we can have full assurance of God's will. This process is for our major decisions — common sense should dictate everyday decisions.

Again reservations come to mind. Five Los Angeles young people, worshipping in the old Azusa Street Mission, gained such a 'deep inner sense of God's will' that they sold all their goods, gave up their jobs, and went to Northern India to evangelize a certain people-group. Their mission was a disaster, one of them committing suicide, one becoming a Hindu convert, and the remaining three working their way back to America in a state of impoverishment and bitter disillusionment. A 'deep inner sense' can all too easily not come from God.

What about chance texts found in the Bible? Many call it the 'lucky dip' method of using the Bible. People flip the Bible open and with shut eyes point at a passage, praying for a word of clear guidance. Often this has to be repeated again and again to get something that makes sense — which in itself should sound a cautionary note. This method has on rare occasions helped someone in dire straits, but on the whole is to be discouraged in favour of in-depth Bible study.

The third test is 'an independent witness through an incident or person'. That independent witness could of course come by chance; or could come supernaturally, influenced by either God or Satan.

Christians are eager, sometimes desperate, for guidance. They will flip coins to arrive at decisions, even in important business and career matters. Those who scorn coins may use a card, writing a 'yes' on one side and a 'no' on the other, then after prayer flipping it into the air. Haphazard methods do not come from God, even when 'sanctified' by prayer. Satan's angels are able to determine which side of a coin or card will be up.

Also to be classified as haphazard is the common practice of asking for a sign. The idea is that provided the token or sign has not been influenced by me — an incident over which I have no control, or a person doing or saying something without a knowledge of my quest — it is God's voice to me. For instance, in the book *We Let Our Son Die*, Lucky and Larry Parker tell the story that, when their son died, they asked God to send rain within twenty-four hours as a sign that He was going to raise the boy to life immediately. The unexpected rain came and the funeral was cancelled in high expectations; but there was no miraculous return to life. God does not encourage such superstitious ways of finding His will, and Satan joins in to strengthen his cause of confusion.

Those who rely on feelings and impressions alone, or look for signs and miracles as pointers to God's will, are in grave danger. The enemy often persuades people to believe that it is God who is guiding them, when in reality they are following only human impulse.

How should we as part of our prayer life seek the guidance of God?

Most important is to look to Jesus for our example. There we learn:

• Jesus untiringly studied the Scriptures to learn the truth about God's character and requirements. As His store of spiritual knowledge grew, a grasp of the Father's laws and thoughts proved a bulwark to Him. He could tell instantly what was compatible with God and what was not. And His knowledge of the Bible was so extensive that people were astounded. More than any other person that has ever lived, Jesus could truly say, 'Your word is a lamp to my feet and a light for my path.'[8]

• Jesus revered and obeyed God's moral law. His words were, ' "To do your will, O my God, is my desire; your law is within my heart." '[9] He also said, ' "It is easier for heaven and earth to disappear than for the least stroke of a pen to drop out of the law." '[10] The breaking of one of the Ten Commandments is sin;[11] and Jesus challenged anyone to point out one instance of sin in His life.[12] It was He who had inspired the Psalmist to write: 'My soul is consumed with longing for your laws at all times. . . . I have chosen the way of truth; I have set my heart on your laws.'[13]

• Jesus started every day with God. Early each morning He was in the place of prayer, giving His all into the hands of His Father.

• He made no plans for His own life, and daily received

from the Holy Spirit God's plans for Him, for that day in particular yet also views of future developments. He did not leave His place of prayer until He had every ray of light His Father intended for Him.

• This was the unvarying pattern of His life. He did not wait for an emergency to intensify His prayer life. Every day and every hour He was reaching out for God's will and strength.

' "Go and do likewise" ',[14] as Jesus said. To have a ready perception of God's will we must be like Jesus in these five points. By prayer earnest and sincere, we will be seeking for sanctification by the Holy Spirit. With the sanctification we will receive divine guidance. God has promised, 'I will instruct you and teach you in the way you should go; I will counsel you and watch over you.'[15]

Will you hear a voice behind you?

The Lord's usual procedure with those who faithfully follow the five Christ principles is firstly to impress the mind, secondly to speak by His providences. God's voice is, therefore, associated with the Scriptures, the Ten Commandments; a vital, constant prayer life, the Holy Spirit impressing the mind and divine providences. The impressions of the mind and the force of events would be dangerously misleading without the five Christ principles.

One last point needs to be mentioned, but with trepidation. Its potential for evil is as great as its potential for good. The Bible says, 'Plans fail for lack of counsel, but with many advisers they succeed.'[16] If the above seven points have been prayerfully and faithfully applied but I am still uncertain, what should I do? It could be a great benefit to get advice from the right counsellor.

There lies the rub — where do I find the ideal adviser? I should not ask myself: 'In whom do I have confidence? Whom do I like, someone whom it would be easy to talk to?' Rather should I ask: 'Who is the person in whom God has confidence?'

This person will qualify on the five Christ principles . . . each one of them. In addition he or she will have a gift of quiet wisdom from God. And be a careful, well-balanced person, experienced, having some insight into human nature. 'Lord, give me wisdom as You promised in James one verse five. Don't let me turn to the wrong person. Lead me to the one true adviser of Your choice.' We should pray most earnestly in this matter.

Having found the counsellor who exemplifies the five Christ principles and is equipped with the experience and well-balanced wisdom, I can explain the problem, mentioning also the impressions and providences I have become aware of. Mr Wiseheart — say that is his name — should pose questions until he is sure he has all the facts. Then he should propose that he and I pray together, each having a chance to pray. When he is sure of his own thinking, he should outline alternatives to me. 'You could follow Plan A; the advantages would be PQR; the disadvantages XYZ. Or you could follow Plan B . . . .' He should not urge me to adopt a certain plan. His function is to help me sort out my thoughts and think clearly. I must make my own decision on my knees in my Father's presence . . . and the Holy Spirit might possibly lead me to discount everything Mr Wiseheart has said. Mr Wiseheart is fallible; the Holy Spirit is infallible, my best and truest Counsellor.

Sometimes divine guidance is sought concerning lesser matters, but situations do arise where the things of time and eternity are at stake. This happened to a young man whom we'll call Skinner.

He was attracted to God because of the beauty of the life of Jesus, but at the same time repelled because of sermons describing eternal torment in hell. He liked the gentle, humane Jesus; but how could the Father of Jesus be so sadistic as to require never-ending hellish suffering from all humans who miss heaven?

He read the Bible and prayed, but confusion was never very far away. Why were Christian Churches so divided? For instance, they agreed on the need for baptism but not on how it should be administered or at what stage of life.

'Don't worry your head about theological matters,' a minister urged. 'If your heart is right with God, that's all that matters.'

'To which Church should I give my allegiance?' Skinner asked. 'The one in which I find myself by the accident of birth?'

'Whichever you find most congenial. Styles of worship differ. Let's say noise levels differ, as do levels of stiffness and formality. Whatever suits you best, that's the one for you. But usually the Church of one's birth.'

A worried pause. 'But — if I was born to Muslim or Hindu parents?'

'No, then you must make a major decision; leave your parents' faith. Christianity is the true religion. But if you want to believe in believer's baptism, go to the Baptist Church. If you like infant baptism you've got a range of choices.'

Deepening worry. 'But — which does *God* prefer?'

A shrug. 'God doesn't have a preference. All He wants is sincerity. Choose what *you* like best, but be sincere.'

Skinner plodded on with his Bible reading, devoting hours to it every day. He wondered how broad-minded God really was. In 2 Samuel 6 he found the ark of God being transported on a cart to Jerusalem. The oxen stumbled and the ark slid to one side, ready to topple off. Uzzah, who was not a priest, felt this was an emergency. Strict adherence to rules was now inappropriate; no authorized priest was at hand. He reached out and steadied the ark. 'The Lord's anger burned against Uzzah because of his irreverent act; therefore God struck him down and he died there beside the ark of God.'[17]

God did seem to require strict obedience. Rationalization, even with pious motives, was not acceptable.

Divine guidance was needed. Skinner prayed with all possible earnestness. He clung to John 7:17: ' "If anyone chooses to do God's will, he will find out whether my teaching comes from God or whether I speak on my own." ' He prayed, 'Lord, I do want to obey. I don't want to know the truth merely to satisfy curiosity or to debate with others. I want to do! Please guide; please point the way.'

He stumbled on to his old bugbear subject of eternal torment in hell. A search revealed that some texts seemed to support the torment idea, others an annihilation principle.

What, did the Bible contradict itself? Analysis revealed that while some texts were entirely unambiguous, others were capable of more than one interpretation. Clearly, if God consigned His enemies to a fate a million times worse than death, His character of 'love and mercy' could be seriously impugned. He would have to be a monster. On the other hand, if He allowed His enemies to die 'the second death',[18] such a suspicion need not be entertained. Was the eventual fate of sinners an eternal punishing, or an eternal punishment? Did not Jesus say in Matthew 10 that God 'can *destroy* both soul and body in hell'?[19] Was the fate of the impenitent not to 'perish'?[20] After studying the language and imagery used, as well as the principle of the character of a God of love, Skinner settled on a conviction that God alone is immortal,[21] and that sinners in hell would not be immortal; their suffering would consequently not be infinite and endless. This brought him great relief and a new confidence in God.

He read Jeremiah 6:16: 'This is what the Lord says: ''Stand at the crossroads and look; ask for the ancient paths, ask where the good way is, and walk in it, and you will find rest for your souls. But you said, 'We will not walk in it.''''' How could the Israelites refuse to walk in God's way when He showed it to them? He prayed, 'Lord, with all these crossroads about me, please show me Your ''ancient paths'', Your ''good way''. I vow I will ''walk in it''.'

So began a search for divine guidance that lasted two-and-a-half years. He visited every church that came to his attention, asked about doctrines, borrowed or bought books and took everything to the Bible. Reading the Bible through every six months, he prayerfully sought to compare Church doctrines with the Word of God. Unwittingly he had started with the correct method.

The question of the Ten Commandments came up. Some Churches historically accepted them as God's eternal, unchangeable moral law. Others were antinomian, saying Christ did away with the Ten Commandments. This was difficult. Both sides quoted texts and swore by them. Skinner prayed desperately, 'To believe that Jesus kept the Ten Commandments on my behalf, so that I don't need to concern myself, would be so easy, so much simpler than the opposite. Especially after the way Jesus in Matthew 5 seems to demand an even stricter keeping of the law. But if You require that I in faith strive to keep the moral law, I'm prepared to do so.'

After months of wrestling he said, 'I am saved by grace. By grace alone. But I am saved to obedience, not to disobedience.' Keeping the commandments became a fixed tenet of his faith.

He was praying more than ever, dedicating each day to God, making God and not people his Counsellor. Where he found that human traditions had played a role in a Church's belief system, he shied away. He was avid for the fullness of truth, convinced that perfect truth is to be found in Christ.

---

[1]Isa. 30:21. [2]Matt. 4:4. [3]Ps. 119:11. [4]Verse 16. [5]1 Cor. 6:19. [6]1 Cor. 10:31. [7]Prov. 14:12. [8]Ps. 119:105. [9]Ps. 40:8. [10]Luke 16:17. [11]James 2:10, 11; 1 John 3:4. [12]John 8:46. [13]Ps. 119:20, 30. [14]Luke 10:37. [15]Ps. 32:8. [16]Prov. 15:22. [17]2 Sam. 6:7. [18]Rev. 20:6-9. [19]Matt. 10:28. [20]John 3:16. [21]1 Tim. 1:17; 6:16.

Acts of grace

It was in May, when a mammoth iceberg was grounded in the Newfoundland bay, that Richy was born. His parents' joy knew no bounds. This was their third son — possibly the last child. How they feasted their eyes on his blond curls and happy demeanour!

At the age of six months he was bouncing happily in his baby bouncer when suddenly the elasticated cords which attached it to the top of the doorframe gave way. He crashed to the floor, landing on his head. At the old army hospital Dr Twomey reported a badly fractured skull, and said that the case was beyond his capabilities. The baby was dying. 'I'll order an emergency flight to take him into St John's.' If the storm let up they could have Richy there in the morning.

The morning broke calm and unusually quiet. When they looked outside there was fog everywhere. The seaplane wouldn't be able to fly. In nearly a year there had never been fog there — why that day?

The hospital waited for the fog to lift. At the little church on the hill they prayed — and waited. His mother Karen sat in a back pew, clutching her sorrow and dread to herself, praying for healing, deliverance from death. 'Please, Lord, heal my baby!' That fog filling the bay, stopping the mercy flight . . . .

The words of a song penetrated her consciousness. 'Jesus, the Saviour, the Anchor, man's only hope . . . .'

She prayed, 'Your will be done, not mine,' and peace enveloped her.

The next morning dawned fogless and bright. First there was the flight. Then interminable hours in a hospital waiting room. At last came Dr Sutherland, the neurosurgeon.

'Mrs White, Dr Twomey never asks for an emergency flight unless it's a matter of life and death. Dr Twomey is so thorough, careful, capable. And he urgently asked for this flight. Yet your baby has no internal bleeding. His head is healing nicely. You could take him home today if you lived here. Why did Dr Twomey send your baby? It's a mystery to me.'

Karen felt as though her heart would burst. 'But not to me, Doctor,' she said quietly.

She knew that many are prayed for but not all are healed. Here she had seen a miracle. Dr Twomey had said Richy was dying. Now — 'You could take him home today if you lived here.'

A total surrender of will to God had been made. That had been the best kind of faith. God's will had been to heal.

Jenny adored the deacon — the first love of her life. Sam, more than ten years older, did not seem to notice the light in her eyes. Others eventually spoke to him and hinted at what an ideal couple they'd make — both religious, of the same Church and culture, both quiet, friendly, helpful to others.

They became friends. She prayed that this might develop into something close and precious and permanent. There were indications that cheered her and gave wings to her hope.

After a year Sam suddenly, inexplicably, ended the friendship.

It was hard for her. She mourned as though for a husband. Life seemed pointless. 'Lord, why did You reject my prayers?' she lamented, and for a month could not pray. She thought she must be a poor follower of Jesus — or not one at all. Why else would God deal with her fervent, hopeful prayers in such a cavalier way? Why else deal with her *heart*, her whole life, so callously?

Sam married someone else. Years passed. He was arrested, charged with various rapes and assaults, found guilty and given a prison sentence.

His wife was humiliated and left with enormous financial problems and a child with muscular dystrophy. 'If only I had never met him and never married him!' she sighed to Jenny. 'I was happy when I met him. Now my days are days of unalloyed misery, full of trouble.' Jenny wept with her.

Deep within herself Jenny was musing, 'Years ago I loved a man and prayed incessantly that this might lead to a wonderful Christian marriage. My prayers were disappointed. I felt shattered. Today I pray: "Lord, thank You for not answering that prayer! That was loving wisdom, loving concern and care." Not having my prayer answered was one of the greatest blessings I have ever received.'

Her faith had survived and grown, and her expanded knowledge of God made her deeply spiritual; a comfort, help and counsellor to many at her work and in the congregation.

To her minister she said, 'Actually, my prayers of long ago *were* answered — with a "No", a loving "No"! It took the years to reveal how compassionate that negative answer was.'

'Did you pray those prayers with a "Thy will be done"?'

'I did. Now, looking back, I wouldn't say the words were fervent, backed by a zealous earnestness. It was . . . just a formula, I suppose. If I had *pleaded* with God not to let me marry that man unless it was in accordance with His plans for me, I'd not have been nearly so shattered when the man dropped me.'

'I've learnt a lesson,' said Roy. 'Lots of burglaries take place in our city — by gangs, unemployed people, drug addicts. Every time I left the house I prayed God's blessing on it. Hundreds of times I came back and found everything in order, and I breathed a little thought of thanks.

'One day when we were away from home our neighbour's house was broken into. It had been much better protected than ours. The burglars were expert. They deactivated the alarm system, ransacked the house for things of value, then fetched a van and, wearing uniforms suitable to a removal firm, carried out items of furniture, appliances, boxes of clothing — all in broad daylight. Then they drove off with a friendly wave to passers-by.

'When I heard what had happened a momentous thought struck me. Hundreds of times we had left our home unattended. No alarm system — just a little prayer. Hundreds of times we returned and found everything in order. Hundreds of miracles! Hundreds of answers to prayer! Yet it was all so routine, almost coincidental, that my gratitude lasted only seconds. I failed to see the real, remarkable answers to my prayers.

'Never again will I enter my untouched home without

saying, "A miracle of God's grace." The same applies to my safety and my wife's. Every day survived is a miracle of preservation for which we have prayed. People speak about not getting answers to their prayers — we've had thousands! Call them routine miracles of grace if you will. Some day when disaster knocks on our door I'll say, "Untold thousands of blessings, and one isolated blow!" '

Patricia's faith was unbelievably sincere. Not yet halfway through her teens, she cherished, studied, and obeyed the Bible. She was the only one in her home so inclined. Her conversation was replete with references to God . . . especially His goodness and everlasting love. If she had two of something she'd give one to someone impoverished, much to her mother's chagrin!

Prayer was her life. She was a rare seeker for God's will. Ravenous for truth, she pleaded for heavenly light from a wholehearted desire to obey. As the Holy Spirit led her into a fuller knowledge of God and His law, she obeyed and was baptized.

Her life was one continuous marvel of witnessing for Christ. Given half a chance she served everyone: cleaning house for an infirm widow, doing shopping for an invalid, encouraging the distressed, giving Bible studies, praying with people. She lived her witness in her home; but her father, mother and brother could not be moved to surrender their hearts to God. They not only resisted her witness but mocked her and in other ways made life hard for her.

'I'd give my life for their conversion!' she said. 'Jesus gave His life for me. I'd give mine without hesitation for Him — and for the conversion of my loved ones.'

Two months before Patricia's 19th birthday her mother stopped the car to let her out for another day's work.

'Mum,' Patricia sighed, 'couldn't we just have a word of prayer?'

'Stop your nonsense,' her mother responded. 'I'll pick you up at five. Make sure you're here.'

'Thank you, dear Mum. May the Lord go with you and bless you.' Such expressions from her were always heartfelt.

Patricia was slightly early to meet her Mum at five o'clock, so she crossed the busy road to speak a word of cheer to an estate agent and his wife.

After a while she said, 'I must go now. I have to meet my Mum on the other side of the road. May God be with you both and bless you!'

She was halfway across when a speeding car struck her and flung her a surprising distance down the road. She died of multiple injuries.

At her funeral her free-thinking father asked me for a chance to say something. 'Always, every day, all the time, she was an angel!' he wept. 'And we persecuted her. Yet she loved us. "I am praying for you, dear Dad", she would tell me. She looked once at some lilies I was growing, and said, "Dad, how will it be in heaven when there is already so much beauty in this broken world?" It was always like that — the words "God" and "Jesus" and "heaven" were constantly on her lips. She was an angel of God! An angel of God!'

He and his wife and their son gave their hearts to God and were baptized.

This praying girl had given everything, and her fondest prayer had been answered.

The bad news came over the telephone. 'Jane was flown down by chartered plane yesterday. She was unconscious. A tumour of the brain. Far too dangerous for her hospital to handle. Here she's in the best hands in the country.'

I stopped at the world-famous hospital half an hour later and was soon speaking to the sister in charge. 'Jane seems fine at the moment, but tests show a sizeable tumour in a bad place.'

'Will there be an operation soon?'

She looked dubious. 'Not here. The neurosurgeons feel this is beyond them. They think she should be flown to a certain specialist in America.'

In sombre mood I walked into the room where Jane lay in a bed with the protective sides up. She looked normal and greeted me with a smile.

'I'm deeply shocked,' I said.

'I'm sorry to be a nuisance.' Her voice was barely audible.

'How did this happen?'

'I was on duty at my hospital when I collapsed.'

'You're looking well.'

She smiled. I leaned my elbows on the bed sides and wondered why they were in position. She knew about the tests, the likelihood of an American phase to her treatment; and with her medical training understood the implications. Deeply moved, I asked if she wished to have prayer with anointing.

'Oh, yes, please!'

'How would 12.30 or one o'clock today be?' She was obviously very eager.

Then, in a heart-stopping moment, her face contorted and her body went into alarming spasms. She convulsed backwards, jerked, flapped against the cot-sides, while foaming at the mouth.

I rushed to the sister. Within moments five nurses were with Jane behind a closed door.

Five hours later I returned and the sister told me, 'When she goes into spasms she seems intent on destroying herself. We sedated her. She's all right now. You can go in.'

The two men whom I had brought along followed me to Jane's side. She was awake, very pale, and could hardly smile in welcome. We prayed earnestly and anointed her. '*If* it is the divine will,' we pleaded, and left her in God's hands.

At 5am the next morning I left for a distant city to serve as speaker at a youth congress. The congress prayed for Jane.

Back home a week later my first thought was to visit Jane if she was still in the country.

I was fortunate enough to find the same ward sister. 'A remarkable thing happened after that prayer service you held for Jane,' she said. 'First, no more convulsions. After a day she looked so well that a new round of tests was called for. You won't believe this, but there was no sign of a tumour! In nearly twenty years of nursing I've never seen anything remotely like this. Jane was discharged, flew back home, and is back at work as ward sister.'

The words of Jesus in the garden of Gethsemane were: 'Father, every thing is possible for you. Take this cup from me. Yet not what I will, but what you will.' The 'cup' was not removed.

But with Jane it was the Father's will to remove it.

Sylvia's operation for breast cancer was not a success and nearly three years of chemotherapy followed while she tried to maintain her normal working life in an insurance office. She had for some twenty years been a fervent follower of Jesus Christ. Having said 'No' to the persistent pleas of marriage by a man who did not share her spiritual priorities, she had made Jesus the Man of her life.

I had often prayed with her, asking for her healing if it was God's will. Several hundred fellow-believers had done the same. Sylvia was totally committed to God's will, and in her own prayers never failed to stipulate that God's wise and loving counsels should prevail.

When at last she was in hospital, her life ebbing away, news of her cheerful courage reached radio broadcasters who were researching a programme on dying. Her permission was sought for an interview. 'Sylvia, tell our listeners something about yourself,' was the first request.

She told of life as an only child, her love for her parents. Then of her yearning for God, her prayers, her discoveries and the momentous decision to follow her Lord with every ounce of her energy as long as she lived.

'Now you have a terminal disease. You know it is terminal, don't you?'

'Of course. But I have already died once, when I died to self and sin and could say with the Apostle Paul, "I am crucified with Christ". So dying is not new to me.'

'How do you feel about . . . dying of cancer?'

'I think it is a great privilege to have a terminal disease. Others suffer unexpected fatal accidents. In a moment, without warning, they are launched into eternity. This cancer gave me ample warning. I could put my affairs in order, particularly my spiritual affairs. Yes, it is a great *privilege* to die of a terminal disease.'

'But aren't you . . . afraid?'

'Perfect love casts out fear. My heavenly Father loves me and I love Him. Why should I fear? After forty-six years I am going to sleep. The next thing I will know will be when Jesus comes, His second advent. He will wake me from sleep and say, "Come, beloved of my Father, inherit the kingdom prepared for you from the foundation of the world!" I will be with Him for ever!'

Not only were the words impressive. The quiet voice with its undertones of faith and fervour was deeply moving.

She fell asleep — triumphantly so. The 'cup' had not been deferred for a few more years in a troubled world.

I shall always remember the comfort Sylvia had derived from the words: 'Precious in the sight of the Lord is the death of his saints.'[1]

It had been revealed to John the Baptist that the Messiah would approach him for baptism, and that a sign of His divine character would then be given.

When Jesus came, John saw in Him a purity of character such as he had never encountered. As Jesus asked for baptism, John drew back and exclaimed, 'You should baptize me!' Jesus insisted, setting an example in fulfilling every requirement of God; and John led the Saviour down into the Jordan and in the name of God lowered Him in spiritual burial beneath the water. As Jesus knelt on the river bank the sign came — the Holy Spirit's descent and the voice from heaven. 'There is the Lamb of God who bears the sins of the world,' John proclaimed.

John was a fearless reprover of sin; this caused him to be arrested and imprisoned. For a free spirit to be shackled in a dark dungeon, breathing foul air night and day, was a nightmare. John's consolation lay in prayerful communion with the Father. His disciples prayed for his safety and release. Jesus prayed for him but did not visit him because this constituted a trap baited by Satan to cut short the mission of the Saviour. John prayed for himself. Months passed. John's health suffered, but he preserved his faith in God.

His disciples came with hearts bleeding for him, but with words that were like knives twisted in a wound. 'Master, if Jesus is the Messiah, why doesn't He deliver you, His forerunner, or at least visit you, as any friend would do? Is He the Messiah — is He?'

'Go and put the question to Him yourselves,' John sighed, concerned for the faith of his friends. Although cruelly tempted, he did not surrender his faith in Jesus Christ.

'Do you people think John is a reed, shaken this way and that by the wind?' Jesus asked. 'Let me tell you, of all men ever born none has been greater in God's sight than John the Baptist.'

Jesus kept on praying for John.

Then . . . the drunken king, slurring the words: 'Go down to John with a sword. Take his head off. Bring it here on a tray.'

While the angels of God watched in horror and agony and were denied permission to intervene, this gruesome, devilish thing was done to a most precious man of God.

When Job's sons and daughters died unexpectedly in one fell swoop of violence, Job said, 'The Lord gave and the Lord has taken away. May the name of the Lord be praised.'

John will live for ever. His immortal faith in God still inspires untold millions of Christians to have faith in God *and in His will.*

About thirteen years had passed since the crucifixion of Christ. King Herod Agrippa I, anxious to be thought a devoted Jew, decided to persecute the Christians in Jerusalem. He set his soldiers to spoiling the houses and other property of Christians, and had James the brother of John killed with the sword. This pleased the Jews, who resented the rapid growth of the Christian community.

Goaded by his increase in popularity, Herod had Peter arrested. It had been a mistake to kill the Apostle James so quickly, instead of lingeringly. Peter must suffer more before being delivered by death. Sixteen soldiers were assigned to watch him night and day in an inner prison cell, in four shifts of four each. One soldier was chained on each side of him and two stood watch at the door of his cell.

Humanly speaking, one would say that Peter had no hope of escaping torture and death. Deep in the bowels of the Fortress of Antonia there was no chance of breaking out. Could his friends not perhaps organize a riot in the streets, causing a distraction while breaking into the fortress? No, they were being harassed by the soldiers and watched by spies. Could someone not bribe the guards? The Christians were poor. What about bringing influence to bear on Herod to release Peter? They had no members of such influence.

All the Christians could do was pray.

On the night before Peter was to appear before Herod, he was lying fast asleep on the cell floor chained to sleeping guards. Suddenly a glorious light shone in the cell. The two guards standing beyond the bars of the cell were blinded by the light. An angel of God appeared in the light and stood over Peter. Prodding him in the side he said, 'Get up quickly.' Peter began to sit up and at once the shackles fell from his wrists. Strangely, the two guards remained in a deep sleep in their chains.

'Come,' said the angel. Peter stepped over one soldier. 'Put on your clothes, Peter.' He put on his sandals, slipped the girdle round his tunic and pulled his cloak over his shoulders.

As the angel moved towards the barred door, it silently opened on its hinges. They passed through and for a moment the guards on either side seemed to be staring right through them, with neither moving a muscle. Behind them the door moved shut and was once more locked.

Down a passage they moved, turning corners until they faced the iron gate leading to steps down into the street. The gate opened for them and neither this, nor the brilliant light flooding the room, registered with the two soldiers on duty. The gate shut behind them.

Without a word they moved down the length of the street. Suddenly the angel was gone and Peter stood blinking in the darkness, slowly coming to the realization that he had not been dreaming.

He took stock of where he was and went to the house of Mary, the mother of John.

The prayer meeting froze at the sound of knocking on the door. The leader nodded to Rhoda, who went to the door. 'Who's there?'

She recognized Peter's voice, clutched at her throat and ran back to the main room. 'Peter is at the door!' she shrieked.

'The girl's out of her mind!' someone snorted.

Peter kept knocking. Others opened it — and there was the apostle for whose release they had been praying! They were so beside themselves with joy and awe that Peter could hardly get a word in. Then he told them his remarkable story and they praised the Lord.

'Oh, the depth of the riches of the wisdom and knowledge of God! How unsearchable his judgements, and his paths beyond tracing out! "Who has known the mind of the Lord? Or who has been his counsellor? Who has ever given to God, that God should repay him?" For from him and through him and to him are all things. To him be the glory for ever!'[2] 'The Lord is good to all.'[3]

---

[1]Ps. 116:15. [2]Rom. 11:33-36. [3]Ps. 145:9.

Disciplined prayer

Charlotte Hamlin disciplined herself in various ways. A vegetarian, she exercised daily by speed walking and cycling, intent on building strength and endurance. At the age of 68 she set out from Oceanside, California, to hike and cycle her way across America, and sixty-five days later, with 2,500 miles behind her, she waded into the Atlantic at Folly Beach, South Carolina.

Hulda Crooks, also a vegetarian, kept herself in constant training over the years, and at the age of 90 made her twenty-seventh assault on Mount Whitney, California, the highest peak in North America outside Alaska. She climbed to the 13,777-foot mark and descended on her own.

A man who has achieved fame as a body-builder tells of his four hours daily, six days a week, lifting weights in the gymnasium. His diet, resting times, friendships and work all revolve around his training.

The Apostle Paul says, 'Everyone who competes in the games goes into strict training. They do it to get a crown that will not last; but we do it to get a crown that will last for ever. Therefore I do not run like a man running aimlessly; I do not fight like a man beating the air. No, I beat my body and make it my slave so that after I have preached to others, I myself will not be disqualified for the prize.'[1]

Some people have been prayer 'athletes'. Luther said his work load was so heavy that he could not handle it unless he spent three hours daily in prayer. John Wesley prayed from four to six in the morning and additionally the rest of the day as he could snatch opportunities. Samuel Rutherford started at three each morning. Joseph Alleine decided on four to eight, saying that if he heard men plying their trades before he was up, he felt shamed: 'Doesn't my Master deserve better than theirs?' Robert Murray McCheyne said, 'I ought to spend the best hours in communion with God. The morning hours, from six to eight, are the most uninterrupted, and when I wake up in the night I rise and pray.' John Welch set himself a goal of eight to ten hours daily! Dr Judson enjoyed retiring for private prayer seven times a day, in addition to practising continuous prayer.

Jesus must have been remarkably self-disciplined. 'Jesus went out *as usual* to the Mount of Olives' to pray.[2] He had planned His life, and He worked His plan. 'Jesus often withdrew to lonely places and prayed.'[3] He spent nights in prayer.[4] Cultivating intimacy with His Father was His priority. No pressure of work, no spies dogging His steps, no sluggishness on the part of His disciples was allowed to rob Him of prayer time.

From the start of His ministry His priorities were clear when He undertook a forty-day retreat for solitude and prayer. From a public relations point of view wouldn't it have been more productive to have spent the forty days cultivating the friendship of the priests and leaders of the Sanhedrin? Jesus felt that communion with God was the most important thing on which He could spent His time.

His disciples did not learn the lesson. Failing daily to build perseverance and power in their prayer life, they were athletes grown flabby and short-winded when He said to them, ' ''Stay here and keep watch with me.'' '[5] They nodded and soon dozed off, sleeping through Jesus' agony, the time when He yearned for understanding and intercessory prayer from His closest friends. ' ''Could you men not keep watch with me for one hour?'' ' He asked.[6] How they needed to rouse themselves, nerve themselves! ' ''Watch and pray so that you will not fall into temptation.'' '[7] Notwithstanding His grinding daily schedule of teaching, preaching and healing, He had kept up His devotional discipline — as should all His followers.

Quaker professor Richard Foster says in his book *The Celebration of Discipline*: 'God has ordained the disciplines of the spiritual life as the means by which we place ourselves where He can bless us.'

A disciplined daily prayer pattern is the highest priority in the Christian life.

Prayer involves opening the whole life to God; it is developing a relationship with God. In prayer we learn to lose our lives so that we can find them. ' ''Whoever finds his life will lose it, and whoever loses his life for my sake will find it." '[8] In prayer we learn to put our Father before everyone else, before ourselves, and before everything — we learn to obey the First Commandment. Every inner-chamber prayer should be a new start to life.

Christ has already given Himself for us and to us. In prayer we give ourselves to Him; we accept His love and wisdom, His plans for us — plans only faintly glimpsed through swirling mists, yet trusted. When in prayer we accept His will — sight unseen, with eagerness — full harmony with Him is achieved.

This requires a plan . . . a plan executed with *discipline*. The following might give you something to ponder; it might even appeal to you.

• When you wake up, say: 'Dear Father, thank You for this moment, this thought of You.' Not necessarily in these words, acknowledge God with your first mental stirrings, so starting the day with God.

• As soon as practicable after rising, go to your place of prayer. Do have a place of prayer, familiar with prayer associations.

> 'A little place of mystic grace,
> Of sin and self swept bare,
> Where I may look into His face
> And talk with Him in prayer.'
> — John Oxenham

Don't say, 'I am a night person. I can't think in the morning.' Follow the example of Jesus by faith. After a light supper the previous evening, have an early-morning appointment with God. Learn force of character by emulating Paul's spirit of, 'I beat my body and make it my slave.' Remember our Lord's disciples whose prayer turned into a snore. As we concentrate on Christ, the Holy Spirit will wake up dormant mental powers. In the morning we pray *towards* the unfolding day; we invigorate the coming hours with our prayer. A backward look at night will not do half as much good.

• Take your favourite Bible, bow your head over it and ask the Father to speak to you.

• Open the Bible. Read a Psalm, or an episode in the life of Jesus — particularly from the crucifixion week. Read unhurriedly, seriously, thoughtfully.

• Kneel and pray over what you have just read.

• Adore God, worship Him. Reflect on His character, greatness, goodness, forgiveness.

• Pray for God's work on earth, His kingdom of grace, His truths — especially those trampled underfoot by 'Christian' people and 'Christian' Churches.

• Pray for Jesus to come and your readiness for that day.

• Pray for your spiritual trueness, needs, development in Christlikeness.

• Pray for your temporal needs.

• Pray for the people and causes on your prayer list. If you have an extensive list divide it up, a quota for each day.

• In between or here at the end, wait in silence on God to speak to you. Meditate on Christ. (If God impresses your mind with a thought, don't tell people, 'God spoke to me and said, "John, I want you to . . . ."' Be truthful and humble. Say, 'The Lord impressed my mind with the thought . . . .')

• Give thanks for blessings.

• Rededicate your all to Christ.

The secret of the Christian life does not lie in positive thinking or forcing oneself into new attitudes. It lies in time spent alone with God. 'By beholding we become changed.'[9] 'I consider everything a loss compared to the surpassing greatness of knowing Christ Jesus my Lord, ... I want to know Christ and the power of his resurrection and the fellowship of sharing in his sufferings, becoming like him in his death.'[10]

How will you discipline your mind to continuous prayer?

'My secret is twofold,' said a bus company executive. 'I hum hymns practically all the time, thinking of the words. At times I hum soundlessly, in consideration for others. Secondly, I put in a word for the Lord whenever I can do so without pushiness or tactlessness. These two help keep me in touch, open to God's movings.'

The One best able to teach us to commune with God all the

time in our minds is the Holy Spirit. He is most eager to help; and will do so if earnestly asked.

Many who have established a prayer discipline find there are times when they have to fight a disinclination. Every feeling opposes it. Now is the time to say, 'I will press on regardless, in the love of Jesus.' 'I press on towards the goal to win the prize for which God has called me heavenward in Christ Jesus.'[11] Thus character is built. When we apply ourselves for three minutes in the place of prayer, we usually find a holy eagerness taking over.

'I met God in the morning when the day was at its best,
And His presence came like sunrise, like a glory in my breast.
All day long His presence lingered, all day long He stayed with me,
And we sailed in perfect calmness on every troubled sea.
Other ships were blown and battered, other ships were sore distressed,
And the wind that seemed to blow them brought to us both peace and rest.
So I think I know the secret, learned by many a troubled way:
I must meet God in the morning, if I want Him through the day.'
— *Ralph Cushman*

[1] 1 Cor. 9:25-27. [2] Luke 22:39, emphasis ours. [3] Luke 5:16. [4] Luke 6:12. [5] Matt. 26:38. [6] Verse 40. [7] Verse 41. [8] Matt. 10:39. [9] See 2 Cor. 3:18, KJV. [10] Phil. 3:8-10. [11] Verse 14.

Christ's comfort and joy

The wife of an eminent American was dying of cancer of the pancreas in November 1974. Her plumber visited her six hours before her death and said, 'Missus, you have to have faith. You have to pray. God's never failed me.'

'Tommy,' she said, 'I don't know where to aim my prayers. God is such a mystery.'

It does not depend on the accuracy of our aim, thank God. Our prayers may be inept, more groans than words; yet the Holy Spirit helps us, intercedes for us and makes our prayers acceptable.[1] We only need sincerity and earnestness; and if in addition we are longingly reaching out to our heavenly Father by faith, the rest is done for us.

How glad we are that God is a mystery! To our tiny minds the Creator of all matter and all life in the universe must be unfathomable. Yet He has revealed much to us, through nature, the Scriptures, prayer, the Holy Spirit and Jesus Christ. His character is no mystery to us. God is love: compassionate and gracious, slow to anger, abounding in love and faithfulness, with a forgiving disposition.[2] He delights to be known by us.[3] Really knowing God is such a deep and supernal experience that it brings us eternal life.[4]

All this makes prayer an exalted privilege. Prayer is the way to foster intimacy in our relationship with the Lord. Christ found comfort and joy in sharing His thoughts with His Father. Because He was human He felt the need of prayer. How much greater our need of it!

In these pages we have examined our motives for praying, and the noblest, most spiritual reason for doing so. We have looked at questions like: Why confess? How — effectively — to get peace? When can you quote a Bible promise to God and know it will be fulfilled? What kind of prayer is answered at once? Can you ever insist that God do what you ask? When is a prayer adoration? What does it mean to pray in the 'name of Christ'? What is persistence in prayer? Why didn't the Apostle Paul persist in his plea for healing? What are the elements of true prayer, the hindrances to answered prayer? What is waiting on God? How is it done? How can one keep praying after prayer? Since God forces no one, are my prayers for someone's conversion pointless? What's the secret of joy? When do prayers require a 'Thy will be done' and when would this be wrong? What pointers can I pick up from the prayer life of Jesus? Does loud praying help, and perspiration? Is prayer still prayer when you're not sending words heavenward? If you had to select just two adjectives to describe true prayer, what would they be?

How can you understand the Bible's apparent 'blank cheque' texts? How does one 'watch unto prayer'? Did Jesus ever speak in 'tongues'? Prayer — commands or surrender? Can Satan manipulate prayer? How Christian is prayer-power? How can I discover God's guidance through prayer? Can I plan my prayer life?

Some of the topics raised are not easy and will require further contemplation. Certain suggestions can be put into practice only with much prayer, faith and perseverance.

One of the greatest needs Christians have is the ability to think critically. They need to be able to assess a matter, analyse, compare with a sound knowledge and interpretation of the Bible, and arrive at an evaluation that *agrees with God's mind.*

There is a great eagerness for information on prayer. When that eagerness is probed the motive uncovered is nearly always: 'How can I pray in such a way that I get what I want? What formula moves God to say "yes"?' The formula usually offered is faith — just believe strongly enough and you'll get what you want. Another procedure is wrestling-with-God-and-storming-the-gates-of-heaven — strong emotions, preferably with sound effects! Yet another is insistence, shying away from submission to God. Texts are taken out of context, with spectacular results — instead of balancing them with other prayer texts, a much safer way of arriving at God's thoughts.

True prayer and a true understanding of God go together. We cannot go by intuition or impressions — of God, people, or topics. We need carefully gathered biblical facts, correctly understood: bench-marks, established principles which can throw light on the less-clear aspects of prayer. These chapters have essayed to provide such norms and tests.

In the end we come back to Jesus and say, 'Lord, teach us to pray!' There we find no prayer techniques that focus attention on self. We find no extremism, no fanaticism. We find instead, 'Not my will, but Thine be done.' Prayer for Christ was not the outlining of a plan of action for God to follow, but the means by which He ascertained the Father's plan so that He could follow it. Christ's prayers kept His mind in perfect harmony with the Father's.

Through prayer we open our hearts wide — to receive Christ our Lord!

> 'I know not by what methods rare,
> But this I know, God answers prayer.
> I know that He has given His Word,
> Which tells me prayer is always heard
> And will be answered soon or late.
> And so I pray and calmly wait.
> I know not if the blessing sought
> Will come in just the way I thought;
> But leave my prayers with Him alone
> Whose will is wiser than my own,
> Assured that He will grant my quest
> Or send some answer far more blest.'
> — *Eliza M. Hickok*

---

[1]Rom. 8:26, 27. [2]1 John 4:8; Exod. 34:6, 7. [3]Jer. 9:24. [4]John 17:3.